JACKIE
SEWELL

JACKIE
SEWELL

KEITH DIXON

First published in Great Britain in 2010 by
The Derby Books Publishing Company Limited, 3 The Parker
Centre, Derby, DE21 4SZ.

ISBN 978-1-85983-876-1

Printed and bound by DZS Grafik, Slovenia

CONTENTS

Introduction

I first spoke to Jack Sewell, as he prefers to be known (he never signs himself Jackie), when I was doing the research for my book on his England colleague, Gil Merrick. Jack's quote was never included in that book, as it amounted to nothing more than him saying that Gil was 'a lucky bugger getting his biography done'. I agreed to approach the publishers of *Gil Merrick* to ask them whether they would be interested in Jack's story.

I was amazed by Jack's vivid memory of his life and career, but this amazement paled into insignificance when he showed me his collection of memorabilia. Nothing had been thrown away over the years and his home was a museum to his career, with every possible type of memento on show: scrapbooks, photographs, programmes, medals, caps, shirts, menus, articles and books.

Jack was born in Whitehaven on 24 January 1927. He played non-League football for Whitehaven before signing for Notts County. Between 1946 and 1951 he scored 97 goals in 179 games for County and was described as 'a direct inside-forward of thrusting penetration and speed'.

During his early days at Notts County, Jack Sewell would work the afternoon shift at the pit at Whitehaven before catching a train to Carlisle. With his boots in his bag, he would then make the arduous journey south, changing at Derby, and end up strolling down Arkwright Street and into the Ma Rogers boarding house in the early hours of Saturday morning. If he was lucky, and it was a home game, he would get a lie-in.

His mining background stood Sewell in good stead. Once, after seeing his England colleague savaged by a vicious tackle, Alf Ramsey said: 'If Jackie Sewell had not been a miner's son he would have been split in two.'

Jack became Britain's most expensive player when Sheffield Wednesday paid Notts County £34,500 for him in March 1951. According to press reports at the time, it made him 'the first footballer to be worth his weight in gold'. He arrived too late to prevent Sheffield Wednesday being relegated from the First Division in that campaign, he helped them win the Second Division Championship in 1951–52.

Sewell played for England in the two infamous matches against Hungary. Unbeaten at Wembley in more than 30 years, England lost 3–6 to the 'Magnificent Magyars' in November 1953 and were then trounced 1–7 in the return fixture in Budapest. Possibly the most notable of Jack's three goals for England was against Austria, in the game in which Nat Lofthouse was knocked unconscious scoring the winner and earned the soubriquet 'Lion of Vienna'.

After 164 appearances for Wednesday, in which he scored 86 goals, Jackie Sewell was transferred to Aston Villa for £17,000 in December 1955. He collected an FA Cup-winner's medal against Manchester United in the FA Cup Final of 1957. In all he scored 36 goals in 123 games for Villa. His last club was Hull City, whom he joined in October 1959, scoring eight times in 44 matches. He left for Rhodesia in 1960 in order to coach and went on to captain the Zambian national team. His work in Africa at club and international level helped to lay the foundations for a football set-up that would eventually bring African players into the game at the highest level.

Acknowledgements

As a lifelong Birmingham City supporter this book has not been a labour of love like my previous books, *Gil Merrick* and *Birmingham City – 50 Greatest Matches*, but the task of documenting the life of an ex-Aston Villa player was made much more enjoyable than I originally expected thanks to the subject's vast array of memorabilia, to which he gave me unlimited access. For their good humour and patience, I thank Jack, the late Barbara and his son Paul. My grateful thanks also go to my family: Julie, Holly, Harry, Matt and Ben Dixon, who have allowed me the time and space to write when there were potentially other priorities. Of course, the book would not exist at all without the team at DB Publishing.

Foreword

By Peter McParland

I was just 19 when I made my international debut in 1953, less than a year after breaking into the first team at club level, and scored twice against Wales.

This was the year I first saw Jack Sewell playing for England against the great Hungarian side at Wembley. The names of Puskas and Co. are now part of world football history, but for me that 6–3 drubbing of England is still the best team performance over 90 minutes I have ever watched. Jackie was one of the few England players to emerge with credit, scoring and being involved in the great move that resulted in Stan Mortensen's goal. By the time I first met him, he had made quite a name for himself as a sharp moving inside-forward, initially scoring a hatful of goals running onto the chances created by Tommy Lawton's head. Then came his record-breaking transfer to Sheffield Wednesday. Upon his move to the Birmingham area he set up house across the road from me in Bromford Lane, Stechford, where in those days there was a very popular racecourse. Jack's house was owned by the club but mine I had bought off an ex-Villa shareholder for the princely sum of £7,500. In those days not everyone had a car and that included Jack, so for a period I used his garage to park my first car, which was a Morris 1000 that cost £400 brand new.

This arrangement suited the Sewell family as I repaid their kindness by always being on stand by to get them to the local hospital, where their son, Paul, was having intensive treatment for a condition which I believe was a complication arising from his birth. These were difficult times for

Barbara and Jack and I was glad to be able to help. Thank goodness Paul made a full recovery.

Jack and I got on well for a number of reasons, one of which was us both having connections with Whitehaven in Cumbria. Jack was born in that area and I had a school pal who, as a merchant seaman, was in and out of Whitehaven on board the colliery ship from my birthplace, Newry. This meant we passed many happy hours chatting about our respective hometown ports.

At the time of his coming to Villa Park, we were having a battle at the bottom of Division One. The club's pre-war success hung heavy on the shoulders of many of their players, and despite stars like Stan Lynn, Johnny Dixon and others, the team never recaptured the glory of those sepia-tinted days. We managed to avoid relegation and the following season Jack became part of a solid foundation which ensured that we were well-positioned in the League and set up a good run in the FA Cup.

Jack played a huge part in the Villa team. I particularly remember his equaliser against Bristol City at Villa Park, when his nose was almost on the deck to head my low cross into the net. That in itself was spectacular, but it was also immensely brave, as the goalmouth was crowded to say the least! Luckily he didn't get his head kicked off – it was a real brave effort.

Jack was one of our outstanding players in the 1957 FA Cup Final, along with Stan Crowther, Pat Saward and Johnny Dixon. Although I managed to score two goals, I should have scored as early as the sixth minute when, in attempting to get onto Jack's cross, I collided with their goalkeeper. I chased the loose ball as Ray Wood collected it, as was the manner in those days. I made no effort to pull out of the chase, but it was not a deliberate attempt to injure an opponent, as was suggested at the time.

That day Jack played a controlled passing game with lots of hard work which helped us to dominate the midfield for a large part of the game, moving from 4–4–3 to 4–2–4 to suit the situation. We were very much the underdogs on the day.

'English football awoke to the near-certainty that it was about to witness the century's first Double,' proclaimed *The Guardian* newspaper. 'United, Matt Busby's babes, were facing Aston Villa at Wembley having already won the League Championship and reached the semi-finals of the European Cup before losing to Real Madrid.

'The precocious qualities of this young United team, their high levels of technique, their passing and movement and above all their capacity to entertain had enthralled the nation.'

Indeed, Busby's young side was widely acclaimed as the best British side of the previous 20 years. We were expected to merely make up the numbers at Wembley, although our lightning counter attacks, which featured Jack's trickery at pace and that had served us well throughout the season, had been identified by Busby as a matter of some concern.

I had joined Aston Villa in 1952 after George Martin had forked out the not inconsiderable sum of £3,880 to bring me, nothing but a promising 18-year-old, over from Dundalk. Less than a year later George had been replaced by Eric Houghton, who had scored many goals from the wing in his playing days at Villa Park. He obviously saw something of himself in me and it was under his management that I made my debut. That year we finished 11th and the following season I served notice of things to come with six goals in 20 appearances, including my first goal against Wolves in a 2–1 win at Molineux on Christmas Eve 1953 (a goal they never forgot, as they signed me in 1961) and goals in three successive games against Middlesbrough, Arsenal and Burnley as Villa finished 13th. Nine goals followed in the next two seasons before I hit a purple patch of form, scoring 19 goals, 12 in the League and seven in the victorious FA Cup campaign of 1956–57. Jack and I were drawn together because we were footballers who scored goals rather than the old-fashioned centre-forwards who just scored goals! I finished top scorer the following season with 17 goals and hit 16 as Villa were relegated in 1958–59, but my best season was when I hit 22 League goals and 25 in total alongside Gerry Hitchens as Villa pipped Cardiff City to the Second Division title.

FACT FILE

Full name: Peter James McParland
Date of birth: 25 April 1934
Birthplace: Newry, County Down, Northern Ireland
Club honours: FA Cup Winners 1957, Second Division title 1960, League Cup in 1961
International honours: 34 caps for Northern Ireland, 10 goals

Playing career

Period	Club	Games	Goals
1952–62	Aston Villa	293	98
1962–63	Wolverhampton W	21	10
1963–64	Plymouth Argyle	38	15
1967–68	Atlanta Chiefs	54	14
	Total	406	137

FOREWORD

(Author's note: Peter McParland was one of Aston Villa's greatest postwar goalscoring wingers, but he will forever be remembered as the man who got away with perhaps the most controversial challenge in FA Cup Final history, when his shoulder charge on Ray Wood left the United keeper poleaxed with a broken cheekbone and effectively reduced United to 10 men. It is a pity that McParland is still associated primarily with that incident, as he gave Villa a decade of superb service. On his day he was a defender's nightmare as he weaved his magic on the left wing.)

1

KELLS – THE SEWELLS AND THE BUCHANANS

It was on 24 January 1927 that John 'Jack' Sewell was born into the estate of Kells, near Whitehaven in Cumbria. Tom, his father, was one of eight Sewells and one of five brothers, the majority of whom played football, while Tom was also a sprinter over 100 yards. William, David and Thomas played for Kells, and Jackie and Douglas played for Workington Reds. Lily, his mother, was one of nine Buchanans, five of whom played alongside Jackie for Kells.

Jack remembers: My mum Lily was what they called just a 'housewife', but she was the mainstay of our family. Our modest, terraced house always looked immaculate, even though it was hardly 'well furnished'. She was a great cook, and although we were neither poor, nor 'comfortable' (no one was rich in Kells), my older sister Elsie and I always had plenty to eat. She looked after me and Dad, without either of us really appreciating her I guess, although I think that's true of all mums. She took an active interest in my career and presented me with a whole host of newspaper cuttings and reports when I moved down south. In Kells everyone knew everyone else and everyone else's business – the Sewells and the Buchanans were typical Kells families, and it was no surprise to anyone on the estate when Tom and Lily became engaged.

If you talk about football in Kells then soon the topic will turn to the Sewell family, and it will not be long before Jackie Sewell's name drops off a few Whitehaven tongues. Jackie's rise to fame is something of a fairytale – the story of the lad with dreams whose future became wrapped up in trips abroad, to the Commonwealth and foreign countries, all in the name of football. The fairytale is made even more interesting because it began in the Whitehaven area, which is famous for being a part of the country where rugby league is dominant.

At Monkray Junior and Infants School Jackie fell in love with football, spending most of his time playing with a old tennis ball, which he had done since he could walk. He remembers one Christmas using a woollen pompom as a ball, and so strongly did he connect with the 'ball' and a nearby piece of furniture that he brought the set of drawers and the Christmas tree, which was on the top of them, crashing down on top of him!

At the age of 13 he won his first football medal, captaining the team that won the Moss Shield with Trinity School. Trinity was a rugby school, but the headmaster, Lance Fitzsimmons, introduced football with immediate success. In 1938–39 Jackie captained the school team to the double of the Moss Shield and the League Cup.

When it was time for young Jack to contribute to the Sewells' household budget he went out and tried his hand at a number of jobs in the area:

At the age of 14 I was labouring on a local farm, which was a great experience and certainly helped me develop muscles I did not know existed. Then I went for a less physical role and became a milk boy on 10 bob (shillings) a week. So before I was 15 I had learnt the value of hard work and money, plus that a day's work could start pretty early. These lessons were put to good use when I started my first real job, which was in the mines on the pit top, loading and unloading coal tubs. My mum, like most other Kells mothers, did not want her son to follow his father down the pit, but for many of my friends of the time that is exactly what happened. It was the norm and continued to happen as generation after generation found gainful employment within the mining industries. The mines and the work they provided maintained strong local communities which supported all the people within them, and it was a tragedy when they were destroyed for political motives in the 1970s.

Football rescued Jack from a lifetime in the pits, but those early days established within him some important values which he has carried with him and lived up to throughout his life and career.

In addition, Jack had to live up to the soccer tradition of uncles William, Dave, Richard, Jackie and Douglas, who had made the name of

Sewell famous in local circles. Jackie and Doug, for instance, had been with Workington Reds in their glory days. Five Buchanan uncles played in the team that won the Workington Shield, League Cup and the Whitehaven Hospital Cup.

During World War Two the Kells Centre FC, which was classed as a Miners' Welfare Team, were considered to be the best side in the area, an accolade which was substantiated in 1944–45 season when they won all the major trophies in Cumberland. Jack was a member of that team, although he was also part of the Notts County set-up at the time.

Jack recalls: We had some good players, and two of the lads got a chance to play League football for Barnsley: Gordon Pallister, who was a left-back, and centre-half Jack Kitchen were given trials by Angus Seed, the Barnsley manager.

It was not long before I got into the Kells teams. I was about 15 years of age and was never out of my depth, even though they had some good strong players, some of whom were not related to me, and soon the scouts were beginning to take notice of me. I had played particularly well in a game at Workington, which obviously set Notts County thinking about me, and it was in the October of 1944 that I decided to throw in my lot with them. After all, they were a famous football team – the oldest in the Football League – so for them to be interested in little old me was quite something. There were difficulties, however, for it was wartime and my work had to be done. That meant I had to travel long distances every weekend to play for County – it was a long trip there and back, and everyone said it was too much for a youngster, even though I just got on with it. It had to be done if I was to achieve my ambition to be a professional footballer.

One weekend in 1944–45 I had not received a telegram from Notts County asking me to play for them, which I thought was a bit odd, but in those days as a young man you never questioned anything! If you were told to do something, or in this case not to be somewhere, that was it, no questions asked. The disappointment of not being selected to go to Nottingham was soon forgotten when my availability proved to be advantageous to Kells football club and its local soccer fans. Why? Because it meant I was able to play for them in the Cumberland Cup Final at Whitehaven recreation ground. It was one of my most memorable games for Kells. I remember being carried off shoulder-high as the fans, many of whom I knew personally, thanked me for my part in the victory. I had scored two goals in a 3–2 win over an Army side that included two professionals, one of whom was Ron Suart of Blackpool. It was only some time afterwards that I realised that my uncles had engineered the whole thing by telling Notts County that I would not be available that weekend. While I understood their motivations, I was disappointed by their deceit, which could have caused me problems with Notts County and finished my career before it had started.

The weekend marathons from Cumbria to Nottinghamshire stopped completely soon after this, and telegrams were no longer required once Jackie moved down to the Nottingham area in 1944 to play as an amateur for the Magpies. A job was found for him at Bestwood Colliery, Nottingham, working at the pit top unloading coal. The job was organised through a Notts County supporter, Jackie Lee, who was a shot firer and foreman at the pit. Not only did the Lee family get him a job, but they also provided lodgings for the young eager lad from so far away. Sewell has fond memories of the Lee family:

Jackie and his family were great to me and provided a very stable base for me to get on with my football career – up until then I had always been Jack, but I soon got called Jackie, which has stuck with me ever since.

Notts County were lucky to secure the services of the much-sought-after goalscoring inside-forward. It was at the age of 16 that Jackie first came under the scrutiny of League scouts. Watching one Kells match, Angus Seed, the Barnsley manager, on the lookout for new talent, was impressed by the Kells centre-half Jack Kitchen, whom he signed, but he rejected the young 'strip'.

Jack remembers: It was a heavy pitch that day, and I didn't go so well. They told me later that Mr Seed had turned me down because he thought I was too light.

Three weeks later, however, Jackie was to get his big break.

Chapter Two

NOTTS COUNTY

J ack's big chance came when Jack Borrowdale, Cumberland scout for Notts County, was asked by Major Buckley to run the rule over Stevenson of Workington. In the match Workington were playing Kells, and he liked Stevenson but also invited Jackie for a trial.

I came down for my trial with Notts County not with my dad but with my uncle. Although dad was a miner he was also quite nervous and timid and therefore made himself unavailable to take me from Cumbria to Nottinghamshire. Uncle Joe Beck was married to dad's sister, and he got the job of being my chaperone.

It was shortly after we had won the Workington Shield when Jack knocked on our front door the following Sunday morning. He told us he was sending two players down for trials with Major Buckley: Colin Wildgoose and Stevenson, both from Workington. He considered me to be better than the pair of them and was recommending me to go for a trial.

I had never been out of Whitehaven before, even for holidays, so I was tickled to death to be staying at the County Hotel right next to the Theatre Royal – I was 'boggle-eyed'.

The next morning I had to be at Meadow Lane for 10.30, and I was surprised to find the stand full of people. I met Major Buckley and his dog, a fox terrier called Brin (later I also had a fox terrier). I got on well with Brin, and according to 'The Major' he didn't take a liking to many people. We had to travel by coach to the Rolls-Royce ground for the trial game. It was a Trent bus, and even the driver referred to Buckley as 'The Major'. I went to sit at the front and was quickly told that that seat was reserved for 'The Major' and Brin. Our opposition was the Rolls-Royce team, and at half-time we were losing 3–1, and 'The Major' was quite critical of a number of the players. Fortunately for me, he put his hand on my head and said 'carry on son, you'll be alright'. His half-time talk worked, and I scored in our 4–3 victory. After the game I was told 'Jack, we will be in touch', but I had heard nothing two weeks later.

I did not have the greatest of games, but I had scored and I was keen, so although they never offered me the chance to sign as an amateur they wanted first refusal if any other club showed an interest. They promptly signed me as a professional when I was 17. To me this was the first step on the ladder to a professional career. Talking of my ambition to be a professional footballer, the first professional game I saw was the first professional match in which I played. Because I was so involved in playing whenever I could, I never got to go to see a professional match.

Jack recalls: Like most boys I would dream of becoming a professional footballer and whether I was dribbling a ball around the streets of Kells or kicking bits of coal around the pit I was pretending to be either playing for England or winning the FA Cup. Unlike most boys I achieved my dream of earning my living from playing football and I was extremely grateful to be given the chance to turn my dreams into ambitions. From the moment of signing my professional forms I was determined to play for England and win the FA Cup and as you will find out as you read this book, I was to achieve both of my career objectives.

There would be a huge gap in Jack's story if the influence of 'The Major' on Jack, Notts County and English football was not recorded in this book.

Franklin Buckley was born in the Manchester suburb of Urmston on 3 October 1882. The title 'Major' was not an affectation, and he did have a military career due to the influence of his father, John, who was a sergeant in the British Army and had a training remit for the local Territorial Army units. When Frank (he soon got rid of the 'lin' bit) left school he was initially a member of the First Volunteer Battalion of the Manchester Regiment before signing up for a 12-year term with the 2nd Battalion of the King's Liverpool Regiment on 24 February 1900 at the age of 17. He was promoted to the rank of Corporal seven months later, before becoming a Lance-Sergeant two years on and a Gymnastic Instructor (First Class) in 1903. He was a keen sportsman, representing his regiment in three sports: football, cricket and rugby. But it was football that was his first love, and while playing for his regiment in the Final of the Irish Cup he was spotted by a scout from Aston Villa who recommended him for a trial.

The then Villa manager, George Ramsay, persuaded him to join and on 30 April 1903, Frank paid the sum of £18 to buy himself out of the Army. He was not a success at Villa Park, failing to make the first team, so he moved with his brother Christopher to Brighton & Hove Albion. On 29 September 1906 he made his debut for Manchester United against Derby County but was an understudy to Charlie Roberts, the England international, and therefore spent the majority of his time in the reserve team. He only played three first-team games for the mighty Reds before moving to their neighbours City, where he made 11 first-team appearances in the 1907–08 season before joining Birmingham City, where he earned himself a regular place in the senior side, scoring four goals in 55 games over the next two seasons.

Always on the move, Frank joined Derby County in May 1911, helping them to win the Division Two title and promotion to the First Division in the 1911–12 season. He was gaining a reputation and was described by one journalist as 'tall, heavily built, pivotal, hard-working and forceful when attacking'.

He played once for England on Valentine's Day 1914 when England lost to Ireland 3–0.Whether he was to blame for the defeat or not, he never played for the national side again. Before the outbreak of World War One he managed four games for his new club Bradford City, whom he had joined in May 1914. Buckley became the first person to join the Football Battalion, and because of his previous experience in the Army he was made a Lieutenant before being promoted to the rank of Major. Within a few weeks the 17th Battalion was made up of 600 men; however, few of them were footballers, most were wannabes who wanted to be in the same battalion as their football heroes. By March 1915, 122 professional footballers had joined up. Major Buckley never played football again due to a lung injury he suffered during the Battle of the Somme.

In 1919 he was appointed manager of Norwich City, who were in the Southern League at the time. It was here that he developed a reputation for finding talented young players, which was dependent on him receiving tips and advice from his old Army comrades, who were all former players and therefore knew what they were looking for in an immature player. After a period out of the game he became Blackpool's manager in the Second Division in 1923 after a chance meeting on a train with Albert Hargreaves, a director of the Bloomfield Road side. He was responsible for the introduction of the now world-famous tangerine orange shirts worn by Blackpool players to this day.

Jack recalls: 'The Major' was a strong believer in how important physical fitness was to a player. He imposed military-like rules on the players regarding what we could eat and drink. We were told to have early nights at least two days prior to a match and not to socialise during this pre-match period. We all did as we were told or we faced the fury of Major Buckley. He was a pioneer regarding physiotherapy, and his techniques certainly helped me return to action after a knock in pretty short time.

Once Jack had joined the professional ranks of association footballers and became a regular at the training ground he found that he was no longer 'Jack' and he had fallen victim to the need for the majority of footballers to have their names modified.

Jack recalls: I do not know where it comes from; this desire to give players 'nicknames' or to change their names into more 'friendly' versions. Is it part of the culture of football or is it the media or society at large that demands that George Best became 'Georgie' or 'Besty' and James Greaves became 'Jimmy' or 'Greavsie' I do not know but what I do know is that from the moment I joined Notts County I was Jackie from that day on!

Back to the Buckley story: Molineux was the next stepping stone for Frank, and he arrived at Wolves in May 1927, where he enhanced his reputation for finding players for little or no cost and selling them on at a profit. He introduced weight training to the club and also recruited the fans to report any player that broke his curfew plan. When Wolverhampton Wanderers won the First Division Championship in 1931–32, 10 of the players had been signed by Buckley.

The *Wolverhampton Express & Star* newspaper reported at the time:
By his splendid work with the Wolves he has built up a reputation as a football manager second to none in the country…At the Molineux Ground he has proved himself to be a splendid judge of a player. His ability to find a young talent is unequalled and despite the handicaps with which he is faced when joining the club he has discovered a whole team, which has taken the Wolves into the highest flight.

Jack remembers: Major Buckley was great, but he had some strange ideas. For instance, he did not like the idea of football players being married. He thought that wives might 'get in the way' of players concentrating on developing their game. He also thought that wives would be anxious about their husband's safety and that this might affect his overall performance. God knows what he would have thought about today's WAGs. His style of football suited me; he liked defenders to get the ball forward early and he liked wingers to take on their markers and cross the ball to the central attackers, whose job was to put the ball into the net. Simple eh? He wanted more passing than dribbling.

(Author's note: Of the 40 players in the Wolverhampton Wanderers squad in 1937, every one was a bachelor, which if nothing else proves the ability of the man to get what he wanted.)

After resigning from Wolves on 8 February 1944, an action which meant he was in breach of the 10-year contract he had signed in 1938, Buckley joined Notts County within a month on what was considered to be an extraordinary annual salary of £4,500. His post Meadow Lane career was:

Date	Club
May 1946	Hull City
May 1948	Leeds United
April 1953	Walsall

Frank Buckley died of heart failure on 22 December 1964 at his home in Walsall.

Jack takes up the story of his signing by Notts County: I cannot deny that I had a great game, and I was told that my name would be put before Major Frank Buckley, the Notts County manager. After nearly a season of Notts County asking me to sign and all the travelling back and forth from Cumbria, I eventually put pen to paper and signed for Magpies in October 1944 for a £10 signing-on fee. I received no wages but did get expenses, which allowed me to have professional status. After the end of World War Two, during which no official games had been played, I got my big chance. It was such a relief when the war ended for all sorts of reasons, but for me it meant no more playing as a guest for other teams in friendly matches (Author's note: Jack played for Workington Town and Carlisle United as a wartime guest) – now I had a chance to play in games that meant something to the players, fans and clubs as points were at stake. I was determined to take my opportunity to impress, and I took it in no uncertain terms. How well did things turn out for me? Well, in four and a half seasons I set a goalscoring record for the club, surpassing Tom Keetley's previous total of 98 in a 4–1 home victory against West Ham United. I remember the game well, and it will always be one of my memorable games. This is how the local newspaper reported my achievement:

MEMORABLE MATCH

NOTTS COUNTY 4 WEST HAM UNITED 1
'SEWELL SETS UP NEW RECORD'
BY A.E. BOTTING

West Ham United, delayed by fog on the way to Meadow Lane for today's match with Notts County, made a dash to the ground by motor coach and arrived 20 minutes before the kick-off.

The visitors found fog very thick between London and Leicester, but a party of their supporters, who came by road, met with little difficulty.

County, with Tommy Lawton back on duty, were hoping to maintain their recent run of success, which had brought them seven out of the last eight possible points. The Hammers were unchanged. The crowd owing to other local football attractions was below normal at 27,073.

Notts County: Bradley, Deans, Corkhill, Robinson, Leuty, Simpson, W. Evans, Sewell, Lawton, Broome, Johnston.

West Ham United: Gregory, Devlin, Forde, Parker, Walker, O'Farrell, Parsons, Barrett, Robinson, Gazzard, Woodgate.

Referee: Mr J.H. Clough (Bolton).

County made a brilliant opening move and nearly took the lead in the first few seconds. From Robinson's pass Sewell, with the ball at his toes, went goalwards and turned the pass slickly inside to Lawton, who put Broome through. Unfortunately off-side had sounded – a very narrow squeak for the visitors!

It was all Notts and after Lawton had been narrowly beaten in a desperate race for the ball by Gregory, Jack Sewell swerved in from the right and just missed the upright with a low cross drive which had Gregory beaten. West Ham were seldom out of their own half, and when centre-forward Robinson staged a breakthrough he was easily held by Leuty.

The Notts forwards were in great form on the slippery surface, and their ball distribution was first-class as was Robinson's 'feeding'. The Hammers seldom looked like getting on top and, fortunately their defence was aided by luck more than once. Notts should certainly have established a commanding lead in the opening phases. Lawton rounded off one brilliant through-the-middle run with a terrific drive which missed the crossbar by inches. At this stage the game was very one-sided.

As so often happens a breakaway in the 19th minute gave West Ham a sharp goal, one of the simplest seen at Meadow Lane this season. Outside-left

Woodgate made ground and lobbed the ball into the goalmouth, Bradley completely misjudging its flight. Thus, right against the run of play the Hammers were in front. But their lead was short-lived, for in the 22nd minute Tommy Lawton levelled the scores when he netted his second goal of the season. It came from a long Corkhill lob into the goalmouth, and with the West Ham defence hesitant, Lawton ran on to a loose ball near the far post and gave Gregory no chance whatever.

Notts were so decisively on top at this stage that it was a wonder that West Ham had not suffered a goal-crop against them. Veteran centre-half Walker often rallied a shaky defence and he was the main obstacle to later Notts attacks in which the County forwards were splendidly supported by their wing-halves. Frank Broome nearly did the trick when Sewell squared a centre right in front of Gregory but the inside-left's shot went straight to Gregory – and still it was all 'one-way traffic'.

With the approach of the interval, West Ham came a little more into the picture, but Leuty easily dominated the centre and Bradley was not troubled. Once when Sewell snapped up a Lawton back-pass he drove in a cracker at which Gregory lunged a fist and somehow scrambled the ball clear. County should have been at least four goals in front.

Half-time: Notts County 1 West Ham United 1

Notts re-opened by attacking and from a grand Sewell pass Lawton forced a corner and full-back Devlin headed out for another flag kick from Johnston's corner kick.

It seemed only a question of time before Notts took the lead. Corkhill and Deans cut out the frills and cleared down field with long kicking to keep County in West Ham's half. Gazzard tried a long shot which was safely gathered by Bradley, but soon the County were again at the visitors' end without the oft-threatened goal materialising. Notts were not moving as well as they were in the opening half.

In scoring the County's second goal to put them in the lead in the 59th minute, Jackie Sewell broke the club's individual goal-scoring record of 98 established by Tom Keetley during seasons 1929–33. It was a grand header that did the trick, Sewell giving Gregory no chance when he connected with Billy Evans' accurate centre.

For the first time in the game the Hammers looked really threatening and exploiting their extreme wingers, they kept the County's defence extended for several minutes before Leuty and Deans held up two through-the-middle raids in which Gazzard was conspicuous. The only time Bradley was called on, however, was when wing-half O'Farrell put in a long drive from near the touchline.

The next goal arrived at a vital moment for West Ham were showing signs of a revival but the County, now moving the heavy ball well again, pressed the Hammers for long spells. Notts nearly increased their lead when Sewell hooked the ball in, Gregory clearing off the line.

Lawton's third goal for Notts and his own third of the season was a brilliant individual effort. When Walker miskicked, the centre-forward ran through, had his first shot blocked but recovered and gave Gregory no chance with a lob into the corner. Just after this Johnston missed from close in. Two minutes from the end Billy Evans beat Gregory all ends up with a right foot drive into the net from Broome's pass.

Congratulations to Jack Sewell on breaking the club's individual goal-scoring record and putting the County on top in a very one-sided game. West

Ham were lucky to go in front from a 'soft' goal as a result of Bradley's one mistake. West Ham's veteran centre-half Walker put up a gallant show and gets full honours in a defence that was overrun for long spells. The County should have been well ahead at the interval. This was County's second win of the season. They have now taken 9 points out of the last ten at stake.

Jack recalls the Notts County legend that was Tommy Lawton: Tom was the best centre-forward I ever saw, played with or against, no problem. Not only was he the best there was in the air he had two exceptionally good feet...the man had incredible presence and brought a tremendous amount of pleasure to spectators...I couldn't speak highly enough about the man.

Recalling Jack's time at Meadow Lane, he tells me that there were two great influences in his football life at the time: Tommy Lawton and Major Frank Buckley. Both of them influenced the way he played, his personal life and the history of Notts County Football Club.

Tommy Lawton – Football Colleague and Personal Friend
Tommy Lawton was a Lancastrian who was born on 6 October 1919, and he was a talent from the earliest of ages. His first major achievement was scoring three goals in an English Schools international trial, but as he was not on the radar of the English Schoolboys Football Association selection committee members he was overlooked when the national team was selected and never got another chance to win a Schoolboy international cap.

When his formal education was over he signed for Burnley, who were in the Second Division at the time, and he made his League debut as an amateur at the age of 16 against Doncaster Rovers. Although he did not have a scoring debut, he made up for it the next week when he scored a brace against Swansea Town. As soon as he was old enough he signed professional forms aged 17, and on his first professional appearance he claimed a hat-trick against Tottenham Hotspur. Tommy may have been ignored as a schoolboy, but now he was a much sought-after signature by the bigger clubs. On 31 December 1936 he was transferred to Everton, and Burnley received a cheque for £6,500, which in those days was a tremendous amount for any player, let alone a boy of such tender years. The pressure was on for Tommy at Goodison Park as the Toffees saw him as a successor to Dixie Dean, who was a legend for the club and the holder of a Football League record which still stands today: 60 goals in a season (1927–28).

Lawton had the full set of football attributes: two feet of equal ability, a blistering turn of pace and the ability to head a ball as hard and as accurately as most average footballers could kick it. His partnership with the great Dixie Dean got him noticed by the England international selectors, and he was chosen to play for the full international team against Wales at Ninian Park, Cardiff, in October 1938 at the age of 19. The away side won 4–2, and young Lawton got on the scoresheet with a penalty – imagine the confidence required to take on this responsibility as a teenager! In his next international game England beat Ireland 7–1, and the game is notable for the five goals scored by Tottenham Hotspur's player, Willie Hall, who had begun his career at Notts County. In the final season prior to the outbreak of World War Two (1938–39) Lawton scored 34 goals, but his attempts to take over the goalscoring record of Dixie Dean were put on hold as he joined the British Army, where he was a physical training instructor. Once demobbed he did not return to Liverpool and chose to sign for Chelsea instead. In his first season (1946–47) he set a club goalscoring record with 26 goals in 34 matches, and everything seemed fine. But Tommy was a perfectionist, and he was fundamentally unhappy with the Stamford Bridge organisation, so he put in a transfer request. He was punished by the club and demoted to the second team; however, this did not stop him being selected for his 11th official international appearance against Ireland, and ironically the venue was Goodison Park.

And so Tommy joined Notts County for £17,500 with the Irish International half-back Bill Dickson moving south. His decision to join a Third Division club at the age of 28 was viewed with disbelief. (Author's note: In the 2009–10 season Sol Campbell transferred from Portsmouth in the Premier League to join Sven-Goran Eriksson's Notts County revolution for a weekly wage of £40,000. Notts County were in League Two, and Campbell stayed for just a single game – so lightning does strike twice!)

Tommy's signing brought about a revolution at Notts County: an additional 10,000 people came onto the terraces, and they were never disappointed by Lawton's performances. There has never been a player so revered by the Meadow Lane faithful – Tommy was the definition of the word 'legend'. The way he played the game would have endeared him to the working-class public who came through the turnstiles on a Saturday afternoon. He never shirked a challenge and was on occasions carried from the field of play suffering with concussion because he was able to hang in the air so long and so high that his jaw frequently made contact with a defender as he descended to the ground.

At the time Tommy was reported in the local press as saying: 'I can not forget the day I joined Notts County – it was 18 November 1947. I was playing for Chelsea, and Arthur Stollery was the manager at Meadow Lane. Arthur had been the masseur at Stamford Bridge, and we had been very good friends whilst he was there. Arthur left suddenly after a row with the chairman and he asked me before leaving whether, if he got fixed up somewhere else, I would be prepared to join him? I said yes but thought nothing more about it until I got a telephone call completely out of the blue from Arthur at Meadow Lane. There were plenty of First Division clubs interested, but I had no hesitation in signing for Arthur.'

Tommy created an incredible goalscoring partnership with Jack. Lawton's awesome power in the air combined brilliantly with Jack's nippiness, and the goals began to flood in. Attendance records were shattered, and the resurgence of the Magpies had begun. They finished sixth in the table.

In the next season Notts scored 102 goals, including a 9–2 thrashing of Ipswich and an 11–1 mauling of Newport County, who prior to this nightmare had been unbeaten in their last six matches. County's away record let them down that season, and they disappointed by finishing 11th in Division Three South. A year after Jack had joined Tommy left the club to join Brentford as their player-manager, having made 166 appearances and scored 103 goals, a goal every 1.61 games. He spent four and a half memorable years at Meadow Lane and was reported on his departure as saying: 'Believe me, there were far too many memories to pick out one above another. I made Nottingham my adopted city. That says enough about my feelings for the place. We broke all attendance records both home and away with the support we had at the time. I was one of the few players to gain international recognition while with a Division Three outfit, and while I will not go into detail it is so disappointing to be leaving with so much dressing-room disruption within the club.'

MEMORABLE MATCH

NOTTS COUNTY 11 NEWPORT COUNTY 1

Decades have passed but over 60 years ago, deep in the mists of memory of Notts County football fans, on a cold and wintry Saturday, 26, 843 of them packed into the Meadow Lane ground to witness a thrilling encounter. The result was an all-time record League score for the Magpies as they blasted hapless Newport County 11–1. The visitors were not the pushovers that the score suggests, but they had no answer to the double act of Lawton and Sewell, who laid on an exhibition of how a tall, physical striker and a speedy inside-forward could wreak havoc in any defence. Earlier in the season Newport had knocked the mighty Leeds United out of the Football Association Cup. The pitch was a quagmire and the weather awful for the duration of the game, but the conditions, as is often the case, served to help provide a match beyond compare. After 45 minutes Notts County were leading 7–0 and the scene was set for a record-breaking day to add to the history of the oldest Football League club in the world. That evening's *Football Post* reported that Newport were fortunate not to return home to Wales having conceded even more goals than they did. Their two-page report on the game read:

Though Notts County lost the toss, they made the early running, and how Newport survived was amazing. From a throw-in the left half, Harry

Adamson, flicked the ball past the Newport defender, Bradford, and, with a low shot past Grant in the Newport goal, the ball entered the net off the far post to give Notts the lead. Next up, Tommy Lawton was in the thick of it, but it was Jackie Sewell who found the net in the 18th minute. Lawton found his right-winger Eric Houghton with a perfect pass, who capitally centred for Sewell who headed a brilliant second goal. Sewell scored again in the 24th minute, having had a couple of shots blocked by Grant, who by now was working overtime. Not to be left off the scoresheet, Tommy Lawton was ready to take his chance. It came in the 26th minute. Sewell, racing up the right wing, centred low to Lawton who deftly turned the ball into the net. The beleaguered Grant was hurling himself around within seconds of the restart and had to reach for a well-placed header from the Notts inside-left Doug Pimbley as he desperately tried to slow the avalanche. But despite his efforts, there was no stopping the Notts charge. They were continually pressing and Sewell, taking up a pass from Pimbley, found another scoring position which he celebrated to the full, driving the ball low into the net just inside the far post with the game only 29 minutes old. But the first-half rout was not over. Not by far. A beautiful pass by Sewell to Johnston enabled the winger to beat Bradford and, using his right foot, Grant had no chance with the shot which provided Notts with their sixth goal in 34 minutes.

Within a couple of minutes Grant had to clear yet another shot, but Eric Houghton, who was closing in on goal, crashed the ball into the back of the net. Half-time must have been a welcome relief as Newport trudged wearily off the muddy pitch. But 15 minutes later, the nightmare was to resume. Newport started well enough, but Notts pressed home the advantage with Newport's defence having to deflect a Pimbley shot, and Grant having to scoop up another from Johnston. Lawton was on target *twice before Newport forward Carr managed a consolation goal. By then, however, Notts had banged two more home. When Pimbley passed low inside to Sewell, who shot first time, he again beat Grant on his right-hand side for County's eighth goal, in 64 minutes. Sewell, who was operating with great speed, ran through again, and his shot was parried by Grant. Lawton then lobbed the ball into the net for the ninth goal in 69 minutes. Even then the thrills were not over. Sewell worked down the half-way line, passed out to Houghton whose centre was well flighted and Lawton, meeting it with his head, contributed Notts' 10th in 87 minutes. A minute from the end, Johnston careered down the wing and centred to Lawton who headed in the 11th.*

Notts County historian Keith Warsop says: 'Despite the way it must have looked, Newport County were no pushover. That season they only finished six points below Notts. It is not as if they were struggling at the bottom of the League. It had been a different story a week or two earlier for Notts. When they travelled to Liverpool for their fourth-round FA Cup tie, although they lost 1–0, Notts found themselves playing in front of the biggest crowd that they have so far faced in their history. Post-war football attendances were high in any case, but that day 61,003 made their way to Anfield for the clash.

(Author's note: Just for the record, Notts County's previous best League score was against Port Vale, whom they beat 10–1 in February 1895. Their all-time highest score was 15–0 in a first-round FA Cup tie with Rotherham Town in October 1885.)

The Notts County team on this momentous day was:

Player	Position
Roy Smith	Goalkeeper
Aubrey Southwell	Right full-back
Bert Purvis	Left full-back
Eddie Gannon	Right half-back
Bill Baxter	Centre-half
Harry Adamson	Left half-back
Eric Houghton	Outside-right
Jackie Sewell	Inside-right
Tommy Lawton	Centre-forward
Doug Pimbley	Inside-left
Tommy Johnston	Outside-left

Jack remembers: Tommy found the player-manager's role difficult and joined Arsenal before leaving the Football League scene. He left with the knowledge that he had never been booked or sent-off in any game he had played in, even though he was a physical type of player. He went into non-League football with Kettering again as player-manager and enjoyed some success before returning to his adopted city as manager at Meadow Lane on 7 May 1957. The team were relegated in his first season back in Division Three, and after his sacking he retired. He told me: 'My time as Notts County manager lasted just 11 months and was a complete disaster for both the club and me. It is a time of my life that is best forgotten.' But he was not a man to hold a grudge, and he returned to County for a third time in October 1968 to head up the club's scouting team, but his time was limited to 15 months because Jimmy Sirrel was appointed as manager. He rearranged the scouting system, and Tommy's role as chief scout was made redundant.

In 1985 Tommy had a regular column in the *Nottingham Evening Post*, which helped him survive a difficult period financially. Prior to his appointment, the *Nottingham Evening Post* hosted a Tommy Lawton Celebration Evening, which was held on Sunday 7 October 1984. It was a tribute to the man, and the VIP guest list read like a Who's Who of Association Football throughout the decades:

George Hardwick, Peter Doherty, Neil Franklin, Raich Carter, Tom Finney, Stan Cullis, Frank Broome, George Young, John Carey, Tony Hateley and Alf Sherwood, plus many of his County teammates; Tommy Johnston, Ron Wylie, Eric Houghton, Doug Pimbley, Jack Wheeler and Jack Sewell.

Jack recalls: It was an emotional night, and one in which I took great pride as he was my best friend. I have in my memorabilia a copy of the VIP guest list which has been signed by all the footballers present. Great memories.

Lawton used the media to promote his friend and teammate's international chances with this article:

THE FOOTBALL NEWS, 28 APRIL 1951

TOMMY LAWTON

'I THINK JACK SEWELL WILL QUICKLY GET HIS ENGLAND CAP'

One week to go and the League 'ups and downs' will be over. Another season finished and another one to look forward to – with as much optimism as ever.

What of the campaign just finishing? The outstanding teams of the season are, in my opinion, Tottenham, Preston and Manchester United, in that order. It looks more than likely that Tottenham will win the championship of Division One the season after topping Division Two which, in itself, is no mean feat, as anybody in this queer game of football can tell you. Preston have been playing great football all the season, and are undoubtedly the outstanding team in Division Two. They thoroughly deserve their promotion, and all Meadow Lane fans will have no disagreement on that score. Manchester United have been in the first three for the last few years, through consistent, good-class football. They may pip Tottenham but I doubt it.

Why haven't I nominated either Blackpool or Newcastle as one of the outstanding teams? My reason for this is that getting to the final has a lot to do with the 'draw' and means only five matches. The League position is determined by 42 games, which means sound, constructive football all the season if you are to go places. This does not mean that the feat of reaching the final by Blackpool and Newcastle has been easy. Both teams have put up fine performances, but for overall consistency, I give it to Tottenham, Preston and Manchester United. It looks like being a 'humdinger' of a game at Hillsborough next Saturday when Sheffield play Everton. What a great performance it will be if Wednesday pull it off and my own former clubs, Everton and Chelsea, join us in the Second Division! And also what a great *personal triumph it will be for Jack Sewell, who, next season, should start a great international career by getting his first full cap. In my opinion, he will manage it, for this boy is a born footballer – and a good 'un.*

If Sheffield stay up, the money paid for Jack will have been worth it although, in my opinion, no player can be valued at the amount of money which Notts are said to have received – even if he is a Carter, Doherty and Mannion rolled into one!

What a hard finish for Forest. Three matches in four days in the last week of the season. But I have no doubt that, before next Saturday, we shall be hailing the Reds as champions – and deservedly so.

It has been no easy matter keeping at the top of Division 3 for practically all season, and I sincerely hope we haven't to wait until the last match of the season to welcome them back to the Second Division.

Good luck and good hunting! In addition to playing good football, you've got to be fighting fit and overcome the number one enemy – nerves – if you are to win championships. And from all accounts Forest have had to also overcome a poor run of the ball. All the more merit when they've done the trick, as we're all sure they will.

Pat on the back, too, for Freddie Steele and his Mansfield lads. They have done amazingly well this season – and expended no fortunes on players. I think those responsible for getting Freddie to Mansfield merit the freedom of Field Mill.

Tommy Lawton

(Author's note: Spurs did win the Division One title, but Forest had to wait a further season before getting promotion to Division Two.)

42

Jack recalls: Tommy was a natural as a newspaper man because he knew the game and was a constant source of stories about his career, and his opinions and thoughts were well-respected as they mirrored his playing career. I was best man at his wedding to Gaye, who was the second Mrs Lawton, but she was the love of his life and his rock. When she died he was never the same, and he never quite recovered from not having her at his side. He had a great sense of humour, and although he got old like we all do, he saw the funny side when he was asked to officially open the 'Tommy Lawton' bar at Meadow Lane.

Jack also remembers Lawton playing a part in his greatest goal: My greatest goal was scored in extra-time during the 1948–49 FA Cup third-round tie between Notts County and Plymouth Argyle at Home Park. There was no score as we changed over for the second half of extra-time, and when Eric Houghton prepared to take a corner on the right, Tommy Lawton and I planned a goal. It worked like a charm. As the ball swung across, Tommy went up to head it but let it go. This caught the Plymouth defence on the wrong foot, and I headed the ball into the net to score the only goal of the match.

It was clear from the local press of the time that the Notts County board of directors were in a dilemma regarding the offer for Jack's services from Sheffield Wednesday:

Notts County directors, who met for over three hours last night, could not reach a decision regarding the possible transfer of Jack Sewell, their inside-right, for whom Sheffield Wednesday have offered a sum of over £30,000.

*At the end of the meeting, the Chairman of the Notts Club Mr C.G.
Barnes said: 'We have not made a decision, but we shall probably make up
our minds sometime tomorrow after further information has been received.'*

*Sewell, one of the most popular players of the Notts side, did not know
anything about this possible transfer until it was announced by the press
yesterday morning. It is only a few weeks ago he received a cheque for £750
from the Notts club, his benefit figure after five years with the club. No matter
what the directors may decide the last word is with the player and Notts
County supporters are hoping that he will decide not to leave Nottingham if
the board should accept the tempting Sheffield Wednesday offer.*

*Sewell at 23 years of age is reaching his prime, and already he is knocking
hard at the door of the international selectors. In just over four seasons in
the senior team he has scored over 100 goals and is one of the players chosen
by the Football Association to tour Australia during the close season. Last
year he was with the FA touring team in Canada.*

*Whether or not the County directors are hoping to make another big
capture if the transfer is agreed to, remains to be seen, but this appears to
be the move in view.*

Jack recalls: My transfer to Sheffield Wednesday caused such an uproar
in the County side of Nottingham that the press was full of articles
which were full of opinions on how my transfer was going to damage
the future for Notts County.

Initially, the board of directors of Notts County (Walmsley [Treasurer],
Barnes [Chairman], Cottee [President], Fisher [Secretary], Linnell, Hubbard,
Levy and Edwards) had such bold plans for the club. They signed Tommy

Lawton and others, but then threw the massive potential away. The sale of Sewell was the start of a policy which led to the long-term decline of Notts County. Cottee and Levy were part of a minority that opposed the decision and they resigned after further policy differences in December 1951. In a statement they said the transfer was unnecessary and that 'we lost one of our best forwards at the time when we were trying to build up a formidable side'. They later joined the ambitious committee at Nottingham Forest, and from then on nearly all the progress was on the other side of the Trent. The seeds were sown – Forest would end the decade in the First Division, County in the Fourth. Where would Notts County be today if Cottee and Levy had won and Barnes and the others had resigned instead?

After his transfer, local sports writer Ralph L. Finn wrote this open letter to Jackie Sewell:

Dear Sir

I feel for you; you have a terrible load to carry. When I remember what a record transfer fee price tag did to Bryn Jones and, later on, to Eddie Quigley, I can only sympathise with you though, of course, I join with all sports enthusiasts in wishing you the best of luck with your new team. If you had come to a side playing confidently and well you would have a better chance than the one you are likely to get with an eleven that started off on the wrong foot by setting itself a target of 38 points in a negative endeavour to keep the side in Division One, rather than with any prospect of winning fresh glories. Since the season opened Wednesday's children have indeed been 'full of woe' and you are joining a very dispirited throng. I blame Wednesday for their present troubles – they should have set out to win the Championship and not made a despondent effort to avoid relegation at all costs. I also blame them for paying such a huge fantastic fee for you. You are not worth it. No footballer is!

I wonder why you did not follow the lead set by Wilf Mannion in refusing to be transferred for any sort of amount bordering on the ridiculous and nonsensical? You could have refused to leave Notts. County and thus pleased the supporters even if you had angered the directors.

Thus I cannot quite absolve you of all blame in this latest and most grotesque transfer of all. You were not quite the slave in the market some people seem to think you had to be!

When I have seen you perform I have found you above the average as a footballer, one with a great deal of promise certainly, but a long way yet from international class.

Will they expect too much from you at Hillsborough? Will your colleagues expect too much from you? Will the supporters? Will you try too hard to prove yourself worth your weight in gold? What a load to shoulder!

You have made a bad move, Jackie, even as Bryn Jones and Eddie Quigley before you. You have all to lose and little to gain.

I hope you are the man and the footballer to rise above your worries and fears. I hope you will be instrumental in lifting Wednesday into a happier position. I hope you will get a bagful of goals and play yourself into the England team…but I do wish you had stayed at Meadow Lane.

Yours sincerely

Ralph L. Finn

(Author's note: Bryn Jones was transferred to Arsenal from Wolves in March 1938 setting a British transfer record of £14,500. Eddie Quigley went from

Sheffield Wednesday to Preston North End in December 1949 for £26,500. After Jack's transfer raised the bar to over £30,000, the next record transfer was in July 1955 when Eddie Firmani went to Sampdoria from Charlton Athletic for £35,000, followed by John Charles to Juventus from Leeds United in April 1957 for £65,000. Denis Law went for £100,000 in June 1961 when he moved to Torino from Manchester City. The rest, as they say, is history!)

The *Nottingham Journal* summed up the whole transfer saga in its report of Friday 16 March 1951:

'SEWELL GOES TO WEDNESDAY'

FIRST DIVISION PLAYER COMING IN HIS PLACE
By A.E. BOTTING

League football's most sensational transfer took place in Nottingham last night, when Notts County decided to accept a fee believed to be well over the record of £34,500 for stockily built 23-year-old inside-right Jack Sewell.

Sewell has now signed for Sheffield Wednesday and, although unlikely to assist his new club tomorrow because of an eye injury which has necessitated hospital treatment, he may make his debut against Sunderland on Easter Saturday. In the visiting side will be Trevor Ford, next to Sewell the most expensive player in League football today. (Author's note: £30,000 to Aston Villa, October 1950.)

The County themselves previously paid the highest fee on record when they signed Tommy Lawton from Chelsea at a fee of £17,000 plus a player (Bill Dickson).

Football's new 'golden boy' took the news that he would be going to Hillsborough with the comment: 'I shall be very sorry to leave Nottingham, where I have been most happy, but I have to think of my future.'

While the negotiations, which lasted several hours following a deadlock meeting of the Notts directors on Wednesday night, were taking place, he went for a sharp walk around the Meadow Lane ground and bought himself a cup of tea. 'I wonder what all the fuss is about?' he grinned when evading a direct question as to his outlook about joining Wednesday, where he links up with another former Notts player, Irish international wing-half Eddie Gannon.

Close on the news of Sewell's transfer, the Notts County club announced their intention of replacing Sewell with a First Division forward, about which a statement is awaited.

Several League clubs, including Aston Villa, have been interested in the 5ft 10 in, 11st, dark-haired sharpshooter Sewell. Recently he broke the club's individual scoring record when he reached a century of League goals, and this season he is top scorer with 14. He is the first to admit that he owes much of his present polish to the tuition of skipper Tommy Lawton, but Sewell is a natural footballer, rated by ex-manager Major Frank Buckley when he joined Notts, his only League club, as a teenager from Whitehaven, as one of the great footballers of the future.

His deadliness in front of goal will be much missed by Notts supporters, and he should considerably assist Wednesday in their fight to avoid relegation.

Sewell, widely tipped as a future England international, is a single lad. He has appeared in representative sides, including an England B team, and toured Canada last summer. He will go to Australia with an FA touring team this year.

Sheffield Wednesday had two representatives at Saturday's match with Southampton, and afterwards described Sewell to me as the player most suited to assist them; although at that stage they were pessimistic about their chances of securing him.

Negotiations for this biggest transfer actually began over the weekend and culminated yesterday after secretary-manager Eric W. Taylor renewed negotiations with Notts Chairman, Mr C.G. Barnes, and other directors at the Victoria Hotel, after a fruitless journey to Wolverhampton in an effort to sign Jesse Pye, England and former Notts forward!

Chapter Three

SHEFFIELD WEDNESDAY

Sheffield Wednesday were struggling against relegation from the old First Division in March 1951 when they made Jack Sewell Britain's most expensive footballer by paying what then seemed a staggering £34,500 to take him to Hillsborough from Second Division Notts County.

Jack recalls: I scored 92 goals in 175 games for the Owls, near enough one goal in every two games, which is good by anyone's standards. All of my six caps for England came while I was at Hillsborough, so I am immensely grateful for my time in Sheffield. And while I enjoyed my time at all the clubs I played for (even my short time at Hull City), those days spent with the Wednesday half of the Steel City were among the happiest of my career, which took in four League clubs

(250 goals in 560 games) and a pioneering African adventure during a period of massive change for the continent.

My move to Sheffield came right out of the blue on what I'll always remember as an incredible day in mid-March 1951. I had no thought of leaving. I was 24 years old, settled at Notts County after being there since Major Frank Buckley had taken me to Meadow Lane seven years or so earlier and, with 104 goals to my name in under 200 games since the end of the war, I was enjoying my football. Certainly I was loving playing alongside my mentor, the legendary England centre-forward Tommy Lawton.

After training, I was walking round the back of the stand and making my way out of the ground when Eric Houghton, the manager, spotted me. He shouted me over. 'There's somebody I'd like to introduce to you to,' he said, pointing to Eric Taylor, the Wednesday secretary-manager. 'Hello, Mr Taylor,' I said and turned to leave. But Houghton stopped me: 'Hang on, Jack, Mr Taylor wants to talk to you. When I asked 'What about?' he replied: 'A transfer to Sheffield'.

I told them I wasn't interested and again turned to go, but they walked along with me and, to cut a long story short, we ended up in the Victoria Hotel. It was there, at about eight o'clock in the evening, that I finally signed for Wednesday. I kept saying no, but with the transfer deadline at hand the Notts directors were urging me to sign. They insisted I'd be doing the club a favour, and once Eric Houghton went off to watch a third-team game I was left exposed and my resistance began to weaken.

'Okay,' I said at last, 'if you want me to go I will.' I looked at Mr Taylor and said: 'I hope you know what you're doing.' Always the gentleman, Mr Taylor said he was sure he would have no cause to regret it – and promised neither would I.

All through the discussions, I was petrified because there was nobody to turn to for advice. I wanted to talk to Tommy Lawton, but we couldn't reach him. My mind was in turmoil, and it was only after I'd signed that I realised that my girlfriend Barbara would be wondering where I was. I dashed straight off to see her and explained what had happened.

It was only when I picked up a newspaper the next morning that the full impact hit me. Nobody had mentioned the fee. I knew it was substantial, but until that moment I had no idea it was £34,500 and a new British record. Honestly, I was shattered. I was desperate to see Lawton because Tommy always had the right words for any situation.

Tommy and I had such a good understanding on the field, it was true, and off the pitch he'd been like a father to me. I used to go up to his home on Friday nights, and we'd sit together listening to records. There was no television then, but in those days we didn't need much more than a warm fire and good company to be content – and talking football with Tommy for hours on end was marvellous entertainment. I often stayed overnight at Tommy's, and after breakfast we used to walk to the ground together. Now, I went down to Meadow Lane on my own, looking for Tommy. When I saw Tommy I almost burst into tears. As we walked round the pitch, I pointed to the newspaper and blurted out: 'I don't know what I've done. They didn't tell me the size of the fee! How can I justify that?'

He assured me I'd be okay: 'Just play as you normally do, have faith in your abilities and keep doing your best, and everything will be fine,' he said. He told me to put the £34,500 fee out of my mind, which was difficult.

Incidentally, I don't remember what my signing-on fee was, but it was no more than £20 – a far cry from what players get today with the help of their agents and all that!

I don't remember much about my Wednesday debut, other than that it was at Liverpool on 17 March, and I scored with a late header from a Dennis Woodhead cross. We lost 2–1, our seventh defeat in nine matches. There had been some doubt about my playing because, at the time, I had a lovely black eye as a result of a smack in the face in an earlier game, which left me with a cracked eyebrow. But I wanted to get my first appearance over. The Liverpool fans gave me some stick. Once, when I was retrieving the ball for a throw-in, some woman at the front of the terraces shouted: 'You're not worth 35 pennies!', which made me laugh and eased the tension.

The Wednesday supporters were always good to me, and I remember my five years at Hillsborough as a happy time. It was an eventful period, and there were some good players at the club. I already knew Eddie Gannon, the Eire international, who had been at Meadow Lane. I was aware that Eddie and the other wing-half, Welsh international Doug Witcomb, were intelligent and perceptive players who would both suit my style.

We always seemed to have a forward line that was capable of playing football. Redfern Froggatt was already an experienced campaigner who knew the game; Dennis Woodhead was full of tricks off the field and made excellent use of a very good left foot on the park. Also, as I discovered, some of the youngsters were very talented. Alan Finney was a very good lad, eager to learn, and Albert Quixall, of course, was already the idol of the supporters.

Albert did very well with Wednesday and had a good career, but his failing was a tendency to take things for granted. I often felt that he might have achieved more if he had been a better listener and shown a greater willingness to learn and work at his game. We often had tactical talks in the snooker room at Hillsborough, but Albert was never one for analysis, and I think that's why he didn't win more caps. He was content to go out and play his own way and never quite understood that you couldn't do that at top level.

Eric Taylor called that phase in the early 1950s the yo-yo years. In my time we went down twice, had at least one escape from the drop, and were on the way to our second promotion in five seasons when I left. I never did get the medal I was entitled to. We also reached the FA Cup semi-final in 1954, when we thought Tom Finney was Preston's only serious threat, but found a hard man called Tommy Docherty was the major reason for our defeat. I still wince when I think of the pain he made me suffer that day! The injury I received in that match was at least partly responsible for ending my international career.

TOMMY DOCHERTY

I was just about to score when he tackled me from behind and damaged my ligaments. I was out for six weeks and my comeback was a friendly game for the Football League against Chelsea at Stamford Bridge. It was an opportunity for me to try out my leg, which was heavily strapped. Although I did OK I knew that I would never be the same again.

Tom Finney wrote in his autobiography: 'The Yorkshiremen rarely threatened to equalise, especially after Sewell had been carried off on a stretcher following a fierce tackle from Tommy Docherty. Sewell did manage to come back on, his leg heavily strapped and his movement clearly restricted, but his contribution was minimal.'

I always got a queer feeling when we played the team from Deepdale either home or away. It is not that they were a dirty side, but they were a blight on Sheffield Wednesday. There was a period of two or three seasons prior to my leaving for Villa Park when Wednesday players suffered injuries when playing North End: goalkeeper Dave McIntosh, broken arm; centre-half Ralph O'Donnell, broken leg; and the worst one of all, the injury to Derek Dooley. When Derek was carried off the field we all knew he had broken his leg. While we felt pretty sorry about it, as Derek's goalscoring had put Wednesday on the map, we were sure that he would be back playing the next season. Later manager Eric Taylor told us that he had had to have his leg taken off. For the rest of that day our dressing room was like a funeral parlour.

The following season, 1953–54, I too had a leg injury against Preston. But I was lucky. It only kept me on the sidelines for a few weeks. Derek told me afterwards that when he saw me go down from his seat in the stands he relived his own accident and he went deathly white. But nobody blames Preston players for any of those injuries – it was just the luck of the game. Even so, every time that fixture came around I thought 'Who is going to get hurt today?'

We were fighting relegation when I arrived, and after the defeat at Liverpool on my debut we won five and only lost two of the next nine games. It looked like being just enough to save us, but it wasn't and we went down despite winning our final game against Everton 6–0.

Chelsea escaped on goal average because they beat Bolton 4–0 on the same day and, so I was told later by my England colleague Nat Lofthouse, their cause was helped by a lenient referee who allowed Chelsea's Bobby Smith to score at least one goal which all the Bolton team and the crowd felt should have been disallowed for illegal use of a forearm.

Our consolation was that we promptly won the Second Division Championship in 1952. Derek Dooley came into the team in early October, and he and I claimed 69 goals between us. Derek was a grand lad and even if he was big and awkward, he got goals. It didn't matter how, he had the knack of scoring. Derek himself and the team profited from playing to his strengths. It was a terrible thing when his career ended the way it did in February 1953. (Author's note: After a collision with Preston North End's goalkeeper, George Thompson, in a League match at Deepdale, Derek's right shinbone was broken. A small cut at the back of his calf became infected. Within two days gangrene set in and his leg was amputated to save his life.)

Of course, it also left us with problems filling Derek's number-nine shirt. There was a time when, following his accident, I was persuaded to switch to centre-forward. I remember having a run of six games in the position towards the end of the 1952–53 season.

To be honest, I wasn't keen and told Mr Taylor I would only take on the job if I could do it my way. I stressed the point that I was no Dooley. However, having watched Lawton at close hand, I felt I knew how I could create space and make scoring opportunities for myself. I scored six in six outings, and although the only match we won in that spell was the last one of the season, against Sunderland, I got a hat-trick and a 4–0 victory left us safe after another battle against relegation.

My departure from Hillsborough was as sudden and unexpected as my arrival. One day in December 1955, Eric Taylor rang and asked me to go to the ground, and when I arrived he said someone had come to see me about a transfer. I think I had missed only three games out of 19 that season, and while Quixall and Froggatt were holding down the inside-forward positions at that time, I wasn't thinking about leaving. So I asked, 'What's gone wrong?'

Mr Taylor said: 'Nothing, and as far as I'm concerned, I don't want you to go anywhere. But it's you they want. They aren't interested in taking Quixall or Froggatt.' I suppose he meant Wednesday were ready to let one of us go, and as I was the one that they had received an offer for there wasn't much choice. In any event, as Albert and Redfern were Sheffield lads, I couldn't imagine they would want to move.

'Anyway,' Mr Taylor added, 'the person who has come in is someone who knows you very well – Eric Houghton at Aston Villa.' I suppose going to play for the man who had been my manager at Notts County clinched it. The situation was the exact reverse of that at Meadow Lane in 1951.

The transfer was completed quickly, and ironically I made my Villa debut at Bramall Lane. I think it pleased a few Wednesdayites that I scored in a 2–2 draw against Sheffield United. At the end of that season, United went down while Wednesday went up. I got an FA Cup-winners' medal with Villa in 1957 and I must say I enjoyed my four years in Birmingham. Indeed, it was during my time there that Barbara and I were married. However, the Sheffield days will always prompt good memories, some of the best of my career.

Eric Taylor spent the whole of his working life as an employee of Sheffield Wednesday. He joined the club in 1929 as a 17-year-old office boy assisting Wednesday's first secretary-manager, Bob Brown. Although Eric never played professional football, he spent 16 years from April 1942 to July 1958 with responsibility for the team and proved a more-than-capable manager, his reign culminating in his side winning the Division Two Championships in 1952 and 1956, to exceed the previous status of runners-up in Division Two in 1950. He was responsible for bringing Jack to Hillsborough as well as Ron Springett, who eventually played in goal for England, and he also developed the careers of John Fantham, Derek Dooley and Albert Quixall, all of whom became significant players in the history of the Owls. Eric Taylor also had great ambitions for the club off the field, wanting to make Hillsborough one of the best stadiums in the country, and he worked tirelessly to make it the obvious choice for representative games and Cup semi-finals. He succeeded in this respect, and it was a venue for the World Cup when England staged the event in 1966. When the club was relegated for the third time in seven years in the 1957–58 season, he decided to give up responsibility for the management of the team, handing over the reins to Harry Catterick.

Ironically, it was Jack's teammate Albert Quixall who took over his mantle as the most expensive player in the English Football League when, only two days after asking for a transfer, he joined Manchester United for a new record fee of £45,000. It was Matt Busby's first signing after he resumed control following his recovery from injuries sustained in the Munich Air Disaster, and it was the first step towards rebuilding the 'Busby Babes'.

MEMORABLE MATCH

SATURDAY 25 APRIL 1953
SHEFFIELD WEDNESDAY 4 SUNDERLAND 0

TEAMS

Sheffield Wednesday: McIntosh, Kenny, Curtis, Witcombe, O'Donnell, Davies, Marriott, Quixall, Sewell, Froggatt, Woodhead.

Sunderland: Threadgold, Stelling, Hedley, Aitken, Walsh, A. Wright, T. Wright, Kirtley, Ford, Shackleton, McSeveney.

Referee: J. McCann (Preston).

The *Yorkshire Post* reported:

What a day of rejoicing at Hillsborough – A 4–0 victory to keep Wednesday in the First Division! Sunderland won the toss, and quite early there was a bad error of judgement on the part of O'Donnell. In clearing he put the ball straight to the feet of Tommy Wright, who was in a dangerous position, but his low centre went straight across the goal. Wednesday then had a look in, and Witcomb went ahead to take a pass from Marriott. He swung in a good centre from the corner flag, and Stelling wasted no time in heading the ball behind for a corner. After Davies had pulled up Tommy Wright smartly, Wednesday took the lead after 12 minutes. Quixall put the ball out to Marriott, who beat Hedley, and when he centred Sewell chested it down and shot through from almost off the penalty spot. Immediately after Threadgold had to take great care over a shot from Froggatt.

The Sunderland defence had a lucky escape when Froggatt worked his way almost up to the goalline and put over a low centre. It was remarkable how the ball was scrambled away. After 29 minutes, however, Wednesday increased their lead when Marriott and Sewell developed an attack out on the right wing. Quixall had run into an unmarked position in readiness for Sewell's centre, and when the ball came over, Aitken, in his anxiety, headed the ball into the corner of the net as well as any forward could have done it.

Wednesday were too quick on the ball at times for Sunderland's liking, and they were more or less dictating the course of the game. Woodhead and Sewell started a movement on the left wing that led to difficulties in the Sunderland goalmouth, but as Quixall lifted the ball back into the middle Threadgold just managed turn it out of Woodhead's reach. He got a bit of a knock in doing so, too. Luck was then against Sewell when he received the ball in the corner of the penalty area and shot. Threadgold parried the ball, and it was touch and go even then whether it would roll into the goal, but it went just outside the post for a corner. Then came one of Sunderland's best efforts, when Wright worked the ball in from the wing and shot just over the bar. Wright and McSeveney had now changed wings. Half-time: Sheffield Wednesday 2 Sunderland 0.

Three minutes after the interval Sewell put in a third goal for Wednesday, and the same player added a fourth after 50 minutes. Both were good goals. In the case of the first, he beat Aitken and, to the right of the goal, hit the ball hard into the top of the net as Hedley went to challenge him. Hardly had the excitement died down than the Wednesday forwards were attacking again in a line, and as the ball was put over to Sewell he hit it with his left foot and it kept low all the way into the net.

Sunderland enjoyed a little more of the game than they had done, and yet they were never really threatening. McSeveney twice put the ball over the bar, and then Shackleton tried a shot but was right off the goal. When

Wednesday did attack, the Sunderland defence invariably had their work cut out, but Trevor Ford almost scored for Sunderland. He looked a certain scorer when McIntosh beat his shot away, and as Ford was trying to recover possession McIntosh scrambled to his feet and held the ball. McIntosh then beat away a terrific shot by Tommy Wright, who hit a ball from Shackleton first time. This was about the best shot of the game. Arthur Wright and Kirtley both shot indifferently when favourably placed, but then so did Marriott on two occasions – once when a far-flung centre by Woodhead dropped over to him and then when Sewell gave him a pass clear of Hedley.

O'Donnell took no chance with a centre from Tommy Wright, for when he headed the ball over his own bar for a corner, he must have been aware that Ford was in a good position. Just before the end O'Donnell hung on to Tommy Wright when it looked as though he would score, and then McIntosh twice survived hefty charges by Ford, as he held the ball.

There was so much comment about Jack's move for such a large amount of money, that he decided to tell his own version of events. Below is the article that appeared in Charles Buchan's *Football Monthly*:

Jackie Sewell tells in an interview with L. Edwin Fairest what it feels like to have A PRICE ON HIS HEAD

What is it like to have a 'price on your head' – not as a hunted fugitive but as a much-sought-after footballer who can repay the highest-ever transfer fee only by creating and scoring match-winning goals? To find out, I went along to see 24-year-old Jack Sewell, steel and whipcord ex-miner, at the Sheffield Wednesday ground at Hillsborough.

It was the Wednesday, goal-starved and haunted by fears of relegation – alas, it came to pass after all – who paid something like £34,500 for the not-too-legible signature of the inside-right who had broken scoring records for Notts County, the club that paid a 'chicken-feed' £10 for him when he turned professional.

Black-haired Sewell, nicely built for speed and power, told me he would prefer to be in the open air – a craze of his – and we chatted while seated in the wooden cream-painted trainer's 'cubby hole'.

It was soon apparent that far from causing Jack to be swollen-headed, he is as humble about his high-priced fame as the hordes of sparrows that twittered over the Hillsborough ground. To him, the huge fee is still a well-stretched nine-days' wonder. He told me: 'It made me frightfully nervous at first whether I could live up to the high expectations of a desperate struggling club, but now I have thrust it into my sub-conscious mind. If anything, it acts as a constant spur to me to do my best always – as I have always tried to do in every game I have been associated with. But it has also made me realise more and more that I have still lots to learn – and I shall keep on learning.'

Jack is finding, too, that it can also penalise a player. On the field he is invariably ghost-haunted. Jerseyed flesh-and-blood opponents hang around like wraiths to try and anticipate and check his every movement. Even so, he has amply proved he can outwit them with his quick-thinking and lightning speed off the mark. A Wednesday official publicly stated: 'If we had had Jack Sewell earlier, there is no doubt we should have stayed in the First Division.' High praise indeed. Jack's meditative comment was that it might have been so, but 'no one man can make a team. It's team-work that counts.' He was sorry, too, that his incursion into the premier division was so brief. It was something he had dreamed about all his life. He said he enjoyed it immensely *and found it a quicker-thinking, faster-moving and more scientific type of game than in the lower divisions. As his club, however, are now high up in the Second Division table, he is sanguine that, barring accidents, he will help them to get back to the 'lost' division – even if it is only on a 'photo-finish'.*

Jack stooped to pick up the tiger-striped office cat as he told me of his rise to fame from the days when he kicked a ball around the slag-heaps in the mining village of Kells, Whitehaven, Cumberland, where he was born. He hardly remembers the days when he hadn't a ball at his toe-ends. He was greatly encouraged by his football-mad father, Tom, who was a great local player in his day. 'Dad still insists that I send him the local newspaper reports so that he can judge for himself whether I have played a good game or not.'

Anyhow, Jack became so good a forward that he captained his school team which, in the 1938–39 season, won the Moss Shield and the League Cup. On his mother's side, too, there were keen footballers. Five uncles played in the barn-storming team that, in one season, won the Workington Shield, League Cup and Whitehaven Hospital Cup.

All his relatives were miners, and Jack gravitated naturally to the family calling. He worked at the pit bottom looking after the ponies at first. His fine play at inside-right – he has always played in that position – attracted Notts County, among others, and he signed for them in 1944. He at once moved to Beswick Colliery, to a pit-bottom loading job, so he could play for the club without having to make long journeys.

A 'no trouble' player, the County officials found him very conscientious in his training at the ground between shifts. He revelled in the game and before leaving to join Sheffield Wednesday, he scored 106 goals. Previously the club record for one player was 96. No wonder, then, that the struggling Wednesday were so persistent in getting on their books so fine a player and opportunist.

Quiet-voiced Jack told me he did not know negotiations for his transfer had been going on for a long time. Mr. Eric Houghton, the Notts manager, introduced him to Mr Eric Taylor, the Wednesday manager, who was quite frank in saying he hoped that Jack would sign to help keep his club in the First Division.

Jack was loath to leave Nottingham, where had made so many friends – including, let it be whispered, a 'steady' girlfriend whose charms outweigh the fact that she is not interested in football. There was something of a drama in the signing. The signature was appended, amid both sorrowful and exultant officials, at 8.30pm on Thursday 15 March, a few hours before the transfer deadline. Modest Sewell admitted to me that that hectic night was a nightmare. He hardly slept a wink and recalled that he had not had time to take advice from older players, and especially from the one man he hero-worshipped – that great player, Tommy Lawton.

He was more nervous next morning when he read the newspapers. They variously described the fee as being between £30,000 and £35,000. He still does not know the actual figure!

Later, he heeded Tommy Lawton's heart-to-heart advice not to worry about it, and to forget that the large sum ever existed. He repaid one infinitesimal part of it the following day, when he got the only goal – against Liverpool's two – with a fine header. He had achieved his First Division ambition.

He has another football hero, the international, crowd-pulling Stanley Matthews. He hopes to emulate him, even though he is doubtful about ever being able to equal that mercurial genius. He found it a grand experience to play several times with Matthews on their Canadian Tour. Said Jack, ruminatively: 'You can learn a lot by playing with a man like him. It is a revelation to what heights a man can reach. He and Tommy Lawton are the greatest players I have ever known.' As we strolled back through the players' entrance Sewell remarked: 'You know, I still think it was the deuce of a sum to pay for a player. It is still hard to believe it was for me.' He added: 'I shall keep on trying and learning until some day I may be thought good enough to represent my country and get an international cap.'

Now, even that dream has come true. Sewell played for England, his country, against Ireland, at Villa Park, on November 14th.

SOCCER STAR, 31 OCTOBER 1953

'BRILLIANCE WAS HIS'
JACKIE SEWELL SOCCER TALE, WRITTEN BY LEE MORRIS.

Throughout the years and years of a football life, the marvellous Major of Football has been findin' 'em young and making them great. The Major, in case you don't know it, is no other than Major Frank Buckley, a great trouper, bluff, of the loud, roaring voice, the genial manner. In pre-war days the Major found them in the back streets, in the mines, in almost every place you can find stars and turned them into top rate material for top-ranking cheques. And one of these boys who found brilliance the Buckley way was Jackie Sewell. In Major Buckley's long tour of the football clubs he took in Notts County. There he produced Jesse Pye and later sowed the seeds that led to the present-day Sewell, one-time highest-ever price star. Sewell moved with that tag on his shoulders to Sheffield Wednesday. Nottingham (on the County side, of course, and not the Forest) bewailed this boy's departure. They had watched this marvellous man with great respect and great enjoyment. They were sorry to see him go. Naturally enough. Sheffield Wednesday fans were glad to see him arrive. Naturally enough. Wednesday were starting on a great run of success when Sewell went there – and I mean despite the history books telling you differently. They had unearthed a potential genius at centre-forward, block-buster Derek Dooley, and they had found the brilliant, dainty, confident Albert Quixall. They also had Redfern Froggatt, soon to be an England star.

Hillsborough was regaining its glory, slowly, surely, certainly. And it was built around the local boy discoveries, the bright boys and the big-money signing, Sewell.

Sheffield Wednesday is a remarkably happy club, it has been built out of the history of our football, and because of that it is homely and very much a little home from home. Sewell, rugged, tough, fast and dangerous, fitted into the scheme of things very nicely.

England selectors, forever on the lookout for new inside-forward stars, looked at Hillsborough and not Bramall Lane, where Jimmy Hagan was king of the castle, and selected Sewell. He played for England and served them well. But the 'sweep away the inside-men mania' that has permeated throughout the post-war history of England teams took Sewell with it, as it was to take Redfern Froggatt later and install in his place no other than Wednesday inside-forward No.3 – Albert Quixall. And in that paragraph rests the story of the spotlighted hero of our piece, Sewell. He is playing in a team that has three international inside-forwards. He is (these are the traditional phrases used by footballers and are not my own) 'always likely to be on his way out', and yet Sewell never worries, nor ever plays as though he is worried by it all.

Sewell remembers, I think with mixed pride and wonder, that Wednesday were prepared to gamble an enormous amount of money on his broad shoulders. And more than that, Eric Taylor was prepared to wait a while and let Sewell settle down happily. He used every means in his power, this fine old-style manager, to let the burden of the highest-ever cheque tag rest lightly on Sewell. He was not too critical of Sewell's early shortcomings, nor was he too enthusiastic about his successes. But in Sewell he had a player who was not too hard to handle. Sewell was a big-hearted character who would not let anything hurt or harm him.

Sewell is, frankly, one of the 'other' types of inside-forward. There are the fancy ones (no less effective, mind you, for all that) and the direct, tough types. Sewell is the latter. He is equally at home at centre-forward – the orthodox, fleet-footed centre forward. He reminds us of the Mickey Fentons and W.G. Richardsons of pre-war days, when most centre-forwards were really inside-forwards anyhow and not just good bashers. He is not a pretty-pretty gambler with fortune. He does not believe in Fate; he makes his own, ruthlessly and efficiently. His footwork is fleet and dangerous. He talks in his own typically Midland accent – his football talk, if you see what I mean. It is a useful, actual, factual, down-to-earth sort of accent, too. There is nothing superficial or affected. Football is Sewell's life. He plays aggressively.

I remember he scored a fine goal once when I saw him with Notts County. The ball came loose from a throw-in, Sewell gathered it, and without hesitation started for goal, even though he was inside his own half. A long loose ball to his centre-forward, a quick dash into the open space, and Sewell had the pass again. Then Sewell stopped, put his foot on the ball and stood waiting. The agonised crowd roared for Sewell to 'get shot of it'. Still Sewell waited patiently. The opposition began to move towards him. Then a movement of a Notts County shirt into one of the 'holes' created by the advance party who had gone to tackle Sewell. A Sewell swerve – a short, sharp sweet pass to the Notts County man, and it was ripping towards the *goal. It hit the crossbar and bounced back. And Sewell was sweeping through hell-bent for goal, and he had scored.*

Sewell, like all great players, knows that patience, pacing and placing are vital things that make goals and victories. That is not an isolated case by any means. He scores many great goals and he makes plenty more. He does not make them with great sweeping gestures. So practical is this man that we are apt to fail to notice his hand, his scheming behind the success. But his colleagues do not. I know that they regard Sewell the same way as I do – one of the most under-rated players of his time.

Jack is part of Sheffield Wednesday's history, and here are some related facts:

Fact One:

A crowd of 31,413 saw Jack make his debut in this team:

Player	Position
A. Morton	Goalkeeper
N. Jackson	Right full-back
N. Curtis	Left full-back
E. Gannon	Right half-back
J. Packard	Centre-half
D. Witcomb	Left half-back
J. Marriott	Outside-right
J. Sewell	Inside-right
H. McJarrow	Centre-forward
R. Froggatt	Inside-left
D. Woodhead	Outside-left

Fact Two:

Jack was a member of the squad that got to the semi-final of the 1953–54 Football Association Cup. He scored in every round except the one that mattered most, the semi-final.

Round	Date	Venue	Opposition	Score	Scorers	Crowd
3	09/01/53	Home	Sheff Utd	1–1	Shaw	61,250
3 Replay	13/01/53	Away	Sheff Utd	3–1	Finney Davies Sewell	40,847
4	30/01/53	Home	Chesterfield	0–0		46,188
4 Replay	03/02/53	Away	Chesterfield	4–2	Shaw (2) Sewell Woodhead	21,808
5	20/02/53	Home	Everton	3–1	Shaw Sewell Woodhead	65,000
6	13/03/53	Home	Bolton W	1–1	Woodhead	65,000
6 Replay	17/03/53	Away	Bolton W	2–0	Sewell Shaw	52,568
Semi-final	27/03/53	Maine Road	Preston North End	0–2		75,213

Fact Three:

Sheffield Wednesday hat-tricks or more:

- 9 February 1952 at home against Cardiff City, won 4–2 in front of 42,881, scored all 4.

• 25 April 1953 at home against Sunderland, won 4–0 in front of 45,168, scored 3.

• 20 August 1955 at home against Plymouth Argyle, won 5–2 in front of 31,716, scored 3.

Fact Four:

While playing for Sheffield Wednesday, Jack won four Football League representative honours:

1951 v Scottish League
1952 v Irish League
1954 v Scottish League
1954 v League of Ireland

Fact Five:

Sheffield Wednesday League performance when Jackie Sewell was part of the team:

							HOME					AWAY			
Div	Season	P	W	D	L	F	A	W	D	L	F	A	Pts	Pos
One	1950–51	42	9	6	6	43	32	3	2	16	21	51	32	21
Two	1951–52	42	14	4	3	54	23	7	7	7	46	43	53	1
One	1952–53	42	8	6	7	35	32	4	5	12	27	40	35	18
One	1953–54	42	12	4	5	43	30	3	2	16	27	61	36	19
One	1954–55	42	7	7	7	42	38	1	3	17	21	62	26	22
Two	1955–56	42	13	5	3	60	28	8	8	5	41	34	55	1

Fact Six:

Jack's Sheffield Wednesday playing career:

SEASON	LEAGUE		FA CUP		TOTAL	
	Apps	Goals	Apps	Goals	Apps	Goals
1950–51	10	6	0	0	10	6
1951–52	35	23	1	0	36	23
1952–53	35	16	1	1	36	17
1953–54	33	15	8	4	41	19
1954–55	35	14	1	0	36	14
1955–56	16	13	0	0	16	13
Total	164	87	11	5	175	92

Fact Seven:

Jack's final game for Sheffield Wednesday was on 26 November 1955 at home v West Ham United, which ended in a 1–1 draw (Shiner).

The team line up was: L. Williams, J. Martin, W. Bingley, T. Gibson, D. McEvoy, A. Kay, A. Finney, J. Sewell, R. Shiner, R. Froggatt, A. Broadbent.

Attendance: 21,670

Chapter Four

ASTON VILLA

Jack joined Aston Villa on 2 December 1955 for £22,000, signing once again for Eric Houghton, who had been the manager at Notts County when Jack was sold to Sheffield Wednesday four years earlier. It was a transfer which was completed in record time, with Jack meeting his Villa teammates for the first time at the Grand Hotel, Sheffield, just one hour before the game was due to start. He knew none of them personally, only by reputation, but it did not seem to affect his debut performance. It was a quick return to Sheffield for Jack as his Villa debut was at Bramall Lane against Sheffield United.

Jack recalls: It was one of the busiest days of my life the day I signed for Aston Villa. The eventful day began in the morning when I was at the hotel in Sheffield waiting for the lads to turn up. It is always a nervous time when you join a new club, but to have no real opportunity to meet the lads in training and have a bit of banter made the whole thing even more awkward. Anyway, I was there and for one reason or another they were delayed and I literally shook hands with them – some of them I knew through playing against them – and we were off for a three o'clock kick-off at Bramall Lane. They were good lads and made me as welcome as they could, but they had their own games to think about. Once you're changed and out on the pitch it becomes all about the two points and nothing else and as a forward it is about getting a goal. All forwards like to score in their first match for a new club, and when I put the ball past young Alan Hodgkinson, I could not help remembering that I also scored in my first match for Wednesday. It was particularly pleasing to score as I had not taken part in any Villa practices so did not know their style of play, but once you score, especially on your debut, it 'gets you in' with the dressing room. After that first match, I was pretty sure I would be able to fit into their attack. I enjoyed playing the game, and I must say that at the time I did not notice much difference in the speed of First Division football compared with the Second Division, where I had been playing with Wednesday.

MEMORABLE MATCH

ASTON VILLA DEBUT
SHEFFIELD UNITED 2 ASTON VILLA 2

Rarely has an opponents' goal received a bigger cheer at Bramall Lane than the one scored by Jack Sewell wearing the famous claret and blue shirt of the Villa for the first time. It came at the 38th minute, when he rammed the ball home from 10 yards. It was a simple goal, but credit must be given to Jack for his anticipation in being in the right spot at the right time and for his opportunism. He was showered with congratulations from his new colleagues. He will be a big asset to the Villa attack later on.

Jack was frequently conspicuous with those long, cross-field and down-the-middle passes, in the execution of which he is a specialist. This game did not warm up until the last half hour, and then the crowd got their money's worth. When Derek Pace got a second goal for the Villa after 62 minutes, it looked as though the visitors had a couple of points safely locked up in their bag. Then United turned on the heat. They set up a series of devastating attacks and these resulted in the Aston defenders tending to become jittery. Under such storming pressure goals were bound to come. At the 69th minute the Scot, Bobbie Howitt, broke through down the middle and scored a lovely goal. Two minutes later Peter Wragg snapped up a stray ball and levelled the scores.

Villa could be begrudged of a point. They took the honours in the first half with their more effective methods, but in their second-half revival United had sufficient chances to have brought off a victory. The veteran Jimmy Hagan provided some gems of football artistry and, to the disappointment of United's supporters, faded out of the picture.

Jack Sewell will remember this game not only because he scored in his first appearance for the Villa but also for the appreciation of the crowd when he scored. Many of those in the 20,000 crowd looked upon him as their football idol when playing at Hillsborough across the City. It was a thoughtful display by Jack; he had purpose behind every move. His deep passes enabled centre-forward Pace to harass centre-half Johnson. Sewell's goal was easily scored after Pace had beaten three defenders.

After the match, Sewell had two barricades before him. First, nearly a dozen newspaper men wanted to talk to him, and then there was a host of boys waiting for his autograph. Having obliged them, he went into the manager's office to do a sound broadcast over Post Office telephone wires, and he was then taken by car to Birmingham to take part in a TV sports programme. Such was his busy day.

A year after moving to the Midlands Jack was given the opportunity to reflect on his first 12 months in an interview with Charles Matheson (Mac) of the *Birmingham Sports Argus*.

It appeared in the *Sports Argus* on Saturday 8 December 1956, and the article was entitled:

'JACKIE SEWELL DOESN'T WANT MUCH!'

Ask Jackie Sewell and he will tell you he does not want much more from football. Through it, the dapper Villa inside-forward has seen quite a bit of the world. He has travelled far, made friends in places far apart and has collected honours, prizes, souvenirs – and a store of knowledge.

Being a modest buddy, Jackie says he will be content with a Cup-winners' medal and a League Championship medal. These, of course, would 'look nice' alongside the Southern Third medal he got with Notts County and the Second Division Championship one gathered in during his service with Sheffield Wednesday.

Meanwhile, the chappie from Kells goes his own gait towards a distinctive position in the ranks of the scoring fraternity. He started this month requiring three more 'bulls' to become a double-figure scorer of League goals in every one of the 11 post-war seasons. Johnny Hancocks of Wolves and Stan

Mortensen of Hull City kept him company in that respect to the end of last term. The 'Mighty Atom' of Molineux has not been able to join in since but there is always the possibility that he might, of course. Meanwhile, Mortensen carries on in the Boothferry Park livery.

How many goals has Sewell scored altogether? That's a teaser which I shall not attempt to answer in full, for so many items have gone unrecorded and he himself cannot help out. With Notts County, he got 97 goals in 179 League matches, according to one record, and with Wednesday 87 in 164. In neither case was note taken of Cup engagements. Then, as he made 15 First Division appearances with Villa last season, scoring twice, in addition to his single in the second of his three Cup games. With Villa this term, Jackie credited himself with seven goals in the first 18 matches. So that, up to date, aggregate of League goals would seem to be 193 in 376 matches. This figure can be carried well over the 200 mark by adding goals scored in Cup conflict and in his half-dozen internationals. And then, bear in mind, Sewell got 15 goals on the FA tour of Canada in 1950, plus 35 more on the Australian tour the following summer. Sure thing, Jackie knows how to 'plant 'em' in the net without trying to burn up the netting by blistering power of shot. He places 'em, genteel like.

It was a nice gesture by Villa to make him captain for the day against his old love Hillsborough last Saturday. The one pity from his point of view was that he did not achieve something to match Nigel Sims for effect, that Villa could not bring back a point. I daresay he will keep on 'chuffing' about that. Don't ask for an explanation of the word 'chuffing'. It's one of Jackie's own.

Jack recalls: My time at Villa Park was great and there were many games that were great for the team and the fans, particularly our Wembley visit in 1957 which is the subject of Chapter Five. But over and above those important League and Cup games there were some matches that stick in my memory for different reasons:

MEMORABLE GAME ONE

THE ARMY 1 ASTON VILLA 7
VILLA THRASH THE SO-TIRED ARMY SIDE
(THEY HAD SIX INTERNATIONALS) 7–1

The Army soccer team is suffering from playing too much football. They showed it in the hiding they got from Aston Villa in the 30-year-old annual match at Aldershot.

There were six internationals in the Army side – Duncan Edwards, Billy Foulkes, Cliff Jones, Graham Shaw, Alan Hodgkinson and Stan Anderson – but they played as if they were tired of seeing the ball. It was four matches in eight days for most of them. Edwards, for instance, had played for England at Belfast on the previous Saturday, for the Army at Crystal Palace on the Monday, and is due at Sunderland for Manchester United the upcoming Saturday. Villa, by contrast, had enjoyed the seaside air at Southsea for five days – and played like it. In a lively forward line Jackie Sewell scored four goals and Johnny Dixon got three. But the Army attack was never in the game, not even when Edwards and Maurice Setters switched after the interval. Their only score was by Anderson from a penalty and they were always struggling from the time Dixon scored after only two minutes. Two of Sewell's goals were brilliant and freakish. The first came when Hodgkinson, attempting a simple throw out, dropped the ball and Sewell neatly lobbed it over his head. The other was when Sewell won a race with Hodgkinson, flicked the ball daintily round the 'keeper and back-heeled it in.

TEAMS:

Aston Villa: Sims, Lynn, Ashfield, Crowther, Dugdale, Saward, Smith, Sewell, Dixon, Roberts, McParland.

The Army: Hodgkinson (Sheffield United), Foulkes (Manchester United), Shaw (Sheffield United), Anderson (Sunderland), Swan (Sheffield Wednesday), Edwards (Manchester United), Crawford (Hearts), Melia (Liverpool), Charlton (Manchester United), Setters (West Bromwich Albion), Jones (Swansea).

MEMORABLE GAME TWO

WORKINGTON 6 ALL-STARS 5

On 5 May 1959 Jack returned to Workington to play as a guest in the benefit match for George Aitken, who had played for Workington as a centre-half from 1953 to 1960, making 262 appearances and scoring three goals. He joined from Middlesbrough, and when his playing career ended he joined the coaching staff at the club he had served for seven years.

Attendance: 6,500

Referee: R.Johnston (Workington)

TEAMS:	
Workington	All-Stars
Newlands	Simpson (Newcastle United)
Brown	Ward (Barnsley)
Garrett (Blackpool)	Powell (Leeds)
Sewell (Aston Villa)	Shankly (Huddersfield)
Aitken	Boot (Huddersfield)
Alexander	Farrell (Tranmere)
Jones	Battye (Huddersfield)
Fernie (Middlesbrough)	Broadis (Carlisle)
Clough (Middlesbrough)	Hawkesworth(Huddersfield)
Peterson	Shannon (Burnley)
Perry (Blackpool)	Eglington (Tranmere)

Workington football fans who went to Borough Park to support George Aitken's benefit match were treated to a magnificent display of football by some of the game's leading stars.

Brought in at the last minute because Blackpool's Jimmy Kelly was unable to turn out, Jackie Sewell was one of the stars of the night. He played some brilliant football, linking up nicely with Willie Fernie, Middlesbrough's Scottish international inside-forward. One of the biggest attractions was Brian Clough, the Middlesbrough centre-forward and leading goalscorer in the Football League this season. The crowd was looking for goals from Clough and he did not disappoint them. He scored a great goal after 29 minutes, beating two defenders and then smacking the ball home firmly with a right-footed shot. Minutes later Des Jones, the Workington outside-right, sailed over a fine centre and Clough was well positioned to head the ball like a rocket into the net.

George Aitken, flanked by Jackie Sewell and teammate Gus Alexander, played a brilliant game at centre-half. One of the outstanding members of the All-Star XI was former Workington manager Bill Shankly, who showed that he has lost none of his football touches despite the passing of the years. Bill was playing football before Brian Clough was born. Ivor Broadis, the Carlisle and former England inside-forward who is now on United's transfer list, showed that there is still a lot of football left in him. He schemed and worked with a great deal of success and capped his performance with a great goal.

SCORERS:

Workington: *Clough (2) Sewell (2) Peterson, Fernie*

All-Stars XI: *Shannon (2) Hawkesworth (2) Broadis*

Jack remembers: During my time at the Villa there were three men who had an effect on my career; two of them in a positive way and one in a negative manner. Eric 'Mr Aston Villa' Houghton was a gentleman in every sense of the word, and he was a friend to all the players and much respected by everyone. He was a man with strong principles, which was never more exhibited than when, as part of the Villa team that toured Germany in 1938, he refused to perform the Nazi salute, which caused something of a political crisis. This event followed a similar incident when in the same year the Football Association had instructed an England side to perform the Nazi salute on the basis that if the players did not follow the instruction they would never be selected for the international team again. Regrettably, in hindsight, I suspect to their great shame, the England players complied with the order. To their great credit and under Eric's leadership the Villa side did not capitulate to the Germans' demands.

This is how Eric remembered the incident in Rogan Taylor's book *Kicking and Screaming*:

When we played the next day – we were Aston Villa (against Lowenburg, or somebody like that) – they treated it more or less as an international match. Our manager, Jimmy Hogan, said 'They'll expect you to perform the Nazi salute.'

The FA fella in charge of the England team had come to our manager and said 'We've had a chat about it and we think it would be better if your players gave the Nazi salute to be really friendly.' We had a meeting about this and George Cummings and Alec Massie and the Scots lads said 'There's no way we're giving the Nazi salute,' so we didn't give it. Our argument was that we were a club side and not an international side.

Anyway, they treated us very well, but it did leave a bit of a nasty taste in the mouth, us refusing to give the Nazi salute. The next time they said we'd got to give the Nazi salute, you see, so we had a meeting and said that, for peace and quietness we'd give the Nazi salute. At the next place, I think it was Stuttgart, both teams gave the Nazi salute, so we went to the centre of the field and gave them the two finger salute and they cheered like mad. They thought it was all right. They didn't know what the two fingers meant. But we've been to Germany several times since and they have treated us very well.

William Eric Houghton was born in Billingsborough, Lincolnshire, on 29 June 1910, when Villa were the reigning League champions. He signed in August 1927 and made his debut two and a half years later. In 1930–31 immortals like Billy Walker and Pongo Waring helped Eric to establish an equally eternal record of 128 goals in the top flight, with the renowned shooting of Eric himself responsible for 30 of these. His form did not go unnoticed by the England selectors, who awarded him seven caps in the early 1930s. In total he made 392 appearances for Villa, scoring 170 goals, many of them as a result of the free-kicks for which he enjoyed such a fearsome reputation. He became manager at Villa Park in 1953.

Jack recalls: Our finest hour was our FA Cup Final victory against the mighty Manchester United.

(Author's note: This defeat meant that Manchester United failed in their attempt to win the League and Cup double, which had not been achieved for 60 years. The team that held that long-standing record was Aston Villa.)

But we were continually struggling in the League and eventually, as it is today, the manager paid the price for his players' efforts on the field. The way he announced his forced resignation was typical of the man. My mate Peter McParland describes it particularly well in his autobiography *Going For Goal*:

We had just beaten Hearts in a floodlight friendly when the boss walked into the dressing room and, with tears in his eyes, told us he was leaving the club. It came as a great shock to all of us. He had not said a single word to any of us about going, though he had known for 24 hours. But it was typical of him to keep back the news so that those players bidding for a first-team place would not be upset. 'All the players liked Eric. He's a real gentleman. In fact, he's too nice a chap to be a football manager.'

A Villa fanatic, he lived, slept and dreamed of Aston Villa seven days a week. Whenever he was called on to do a party piece, he would always stand up and sing his Villa song An Old Jersey of Claret and Blue. *After he left, he was offered several thousand pounds by one Sunday newspaper for his story, but Eric refused to get involved in any mud-slinging against the club he loved.*

Eric came back to Villa Park to serve as a director and later became the club's only permanent senior vice-president.

Jack continues: As well as Eric Houghton, another great fellow who was with me at Notts County and also Villa Park was Billy Moore, our trainer. He was a Geordie and like all lads from the North East he was as hard as nails coupled with a great sense of humour. Bill played for Stoke City during the first era of Stanley Matthews. He moved to Mansfield Town just prior to the outbreak of World War Two, and immediately after the conflict ended he was appointed trainer at Meadow Lane. It was there he formed his great relationship with Eric, and he simply became his 'right-hand man' with all the responsibilities that come with that title! But I suppose like all of us Bill wanted to push his talents to the limit, and it was with great surprise, and some disappointment from a personal point of view, when in the December of 1957 he moved to manage Walsall, who were at the bottom of Division Three South.

Bill made the grade and by 1961 they had gained promotion to the Second Division. In 1963, with the Saddlers back in Division Three, he went to Fulham in a scouting role before returning to Walsall in 1969. He stayed there for just over three years before leaving due to financial difficulties within the Fellows Park club. Later Bill ran the Fox Hotel in Stafford before his death in 1982.

If those two guys helped my career, then Joe Mercer definitely conspired to end my stay in Birmingham. We had been relegated and Joe had been brought in to change things, which he did, which included my departure. Joe was a football man; he played for both Everton and Arsenal at the highest levels and had won England caps to go alongside his three Division One champions' medals (with Everton in 1938–39 and Arsenal in 1948–49 and 1952–53). (Author's note: He was also elected Footballer of the Year in 1950.) He was a grocer by trade and therefore knew the value of money, which I guess helped him in his managerial career, which began with Sheffield United in 1955. He stayed there for three years before coming to change things in my life.

Joe Mercer, while making Jack's life difficult at Villa Park, did prove successful for the Claret and Blues, as they won the Second Division Championship in 1960, which was followed a year later by victory in the very first League Cup competition. He left Villa Park due to poor health, but his managerial career was far from over and his halcyon days had yet to come at Maine Road, Manchester, where his trophy cabinet included the Division Two Championship in 1965–66, the Division One Championship in 1967–68, the FA Cup in 1969, the League Cup in 1970 and the European Cup-Winners' Cup in the same year.

(Author's note: Joe Mercer was appointed caretaker-manager of England in 1974, and in a four-week period he took charge of seven games – winning three, drawing one and losing the remainder.)

Joe Mercer was a strong left-half, who starred for Everton in the mid-to-late 1930s, winning five England caps, before his career was interrupted by World War Two. He joined Arsenal after the war, playing almost 250 League games in nine years before retiring in 1955. Mercer played five times for England.

Jack is part of Aston Villa's history, and here are some related facts:

Fact One:

Jack's Aston Villa playing career:

Season	Games	Goals
1955–56	18	3
1956–57	48	18
1957–58	39	11
1958–59	37	7
1959–60	2	1
Total	144	40

Fact Two:

While at Villa in 1957–58, Jack became the only player to score double-figure goals in every season since World War Two.

Fact Three:

In January 1958, Stan Lynn became the first full-back to score a League hat-trick. Lynn's first two goals were penalties and he hit his third goal from a Leslie Smith corner as Villa beat Sunderland 5–2. Villa's other marksmen were Billy Myerscough and Jackie Sewell.

Fact Four:

Jack's goalscoring average for League games was 1:3.4 (123 League games scoring 36 goals) and for FA Cup Games was 1:5.25 (21 FA Cup games netting four goals).

Footnote

Peter McParland, who wrote the Foreword to this book, was asked by the Aston Villa Former Players' Association to select his top Villa XI. His response was:

If I'd been asked to name a World XI, rather than my Villa dream team, two of my selections would have been exactly the same – and not just because, like me, they're from across the Irish Sea! Not many footballers can be described as sheer genius, but the phrase certainly applies to PAUL McGRATH and DANNY BLANCHFLOWER.

I saw Danny at first hand when we played together at Villa Park in the early 1950s, and four decades later I watched Paul from a seat in the stand. And I can honestly say I never saw either of them have a bad game. Blanchflower may have enjoyed almost all his success with Tottenham Hotspur, but his artistry and presence were evident long before he moved to White Hart Lane. He could take a game by the scruff of the neck and dictate how he wanted it played. McGrath, meanwhile, was simply a magnificent defender who simply had no peers. Former Villa physiotherapist Jim Walker used to say Paul would have been just as comfortable playing football in a collar and tie, and you could see what he meant.

Alongside Macca, I have opted for JIMMY DUGDALE, one of my colleagues in the 1957 FA Cup triumph and a player who was desperately unlucky never to win an England cap. My defence also features two other members of the Wembley side, with the reliable NIGEL SIMS in goal and STAN LYNN, the solid defender with a thunderbolt shot, at right-back. My left-back is GEORGE CUMMINGS, whose career was over by the time I arrived at Villa Park. George was both classy and hard – and was one of the few players capable of keeping the legendary Stan Matthews quiet!

Apart from Blanchflower, my midfield comprises another of the 1957 side, plus two men who steered Villa to European Cup glory 25 years later. I would instruct JACKIE SEWELL and TONY MORLEY to attack the opposition from midfield while relying on GORDON COWANS to win the ball and provide the precision passes which were his trademark.

Up front, ANDY GRAY would be a perfect target man with his daredevil approach, while TOMMY THOMPSON, who was like lightning in the penalty area, would be Andy's ideal striking partner.

Chapter Five

FA CUP FINAL
1957

J**ack recalls:** We travelled down to London on the Friday night and stayed
at the Brent Bridge Hotel. (Author's note: The hotel no longer exists – it
was situated at the junction between the A406 North Circular Road and Brent
Street. All that remains are a pair of curious conical summerhouses, one on each
of the river's banks. These are the final remains of the Brent Bridge Hotel, a once-
popular meeting place in the region, which stood on the site of what is now
Woodbourne Close.)

In those days the squad was the first team plus reserves in case any
player got injured before the kick off. There was one major doubt for us
and that was Derek Pace. Derek was our regular number nine and had
been the first choice for the whole season. It was unlucky for Derek, who
was nicknamed 'Doc'.

There were some stirring Villa displays in the rounds up to the Final. One of these was against Burnley, and Jimmy McIlroy of Burnley wrote the following account of their 1957 quarter-final encounter:

Against the Villa, we took an early lead, and without playing really well held it until a few minutes from the end of the game. Then, the most dangerous man in soccer at converting the pass to the far-post, Peter McParland, popped up to head the equaliser from his favourite position. But there should never have been any replay. In the first 10 minutes or so, I squared two passes across the face of the goal, both taken by Ian Lawson in his stride. From very close range, Ian side-footed the ball wide each time.

The pitch at Villa Park [in the replay] was in a shocking state. There were pools of water on the surface, and where there was no water, there was mud – gallons of the stuff! In one corner, in fact, there was a patch of filth giving off a most nauseating odour, causing us to wonder if this famous football ground had been used for sewage disposal. Thus was the stage set in terrible conditions for one of the most vital Cup-ties in the history of either club.

After we had won the semi-final, Jimmy Dugdale, who had played for West Bromwich Albion in the 1954 FA Cup Final, arranged a team meeting in the Villa Park boot room with Eric Houghton (the manager) and Billy Moore (the trainer) about how we were going to raise money for the team in what was a potentially once-in-a-lifetime opportunity for most players. Every member of the team was allocated a job to do to raise money for the players; two lads had to find an official photographer (I think we ended up with two!), and Jimmy and I organised a dance at the Gay Tower Ballroom in Edgbaston. I took on the role of fundraising manager and co-ordinated the agreements, which I guess are called 'sponsorship deals' these days. We had a boot deal which cost the manufacturer £150. For some reason £150 was the going rate for 'kitty' donations. Swallow raincoats did a deal through Johnny Dixon, which was a free raincoat for every player!

We were allocated 1,000 tickets between us, which were mainly terrace tickets with a few for seats near to the Queen's box, wherever they were we saved some for our family and friends and the rest we sold on at a good profit. There was a busload of my supporters from Kells who all got into Wembley free-of-charge!

Jack remembers: Villa were regarded as workhorses by independent observers, while United were thought of as pedigree stallions! Villa were, however, served by some illustrious players in the form of Nigel Sims (goal), Jimmy Dugdale (centre-half), captain Johnny Dixon and the lively Peter McParland in attack. The only player who could be properly regarded as a 'workhorse' was full-back Stan Lynn, who was totally uncomprising in the tackle, as was Stan Crowther (who played for Manchester United in the 1958 FA Cup Final, becoming the first man to legally play for two teams in the same competition).

Aston Villa at that time were being criticised on all sides for their vigorous style of football. They tackled hard, used their weight to the maximum advantage, and generally bothered little with the frills of soccer, although their manager Mr Eric Houghton repeatedly refuted charges that Villa were over-robust, there is no denying they were formidable opposition. In marked contrast, Burnley were a team of flyweights, with one of the smallest forward lines in the entire League. McIlroy continues: *The Midlanders beat us 2–0, with goals coming from Johnny Dixon and, inevitably, my old Irish pal Peter McParland. I say inevitably, because Peter makes a habit of scoring whenever he plays against me. Indeed, he has scored more goals while playing against me than as my partner in the Irish team, even though we have played many more times together than as opponents.*

Burnley were out of the Cup, well beaten on a terrible pitch by an efficient, workmanlike team. The match was not a classic, my main recollection of it being the rather odd-looking playing strip sported by the Burnley players. We wore navy blue shirts and navy blue shorts, and with the referee in his customary all-black outfit it was not surprising that he was given more passes than anyone in our team! We wondered at the time why return passes never came. Fortunately he changed into a white shirt at half-time, although I am still not certain whether this simplified or further confused the issue!

However, McIlroy does not provide the whole story for the dark outfits they wore. Peter McParland takes up the story about this match in the days before floodlights at Villa Park: *It was a foul afternoon. Wet and dark. A really filthy day. So Burnley decided to wear black! With almost no natural light and against the dark background of the crowd it was impossible to make their players out. Eric Houghton, our manager, came into our dressing room before the kick-off raging. He went to see the referee and complain but all the ref did was ask to borrow one of our white away-shirts to wear!*

How Villa got to Wembley:

Round	Date	Venue	Opposition	Score
3	05/01/57	Away	Luton Town	2–2
3 Replay	07/01/57	Home	Luton Town	2–0
4	26/01/57	Away	Middlesbrough	3–2
5	16/02/57	Home	Bristol City	2–1
6	02/03/57	Away	Burnley	0–0
6 Replay	06/03/57	Home	Burnley	2–0
Semi-final	23/03/57		West Bromwich Albion	2–2
S-f Replay	28/03/57		West Bromwich Albion	1–0

Two weeks before the 1957 FA Cup Final, Manchester United (the 'Busby Babes') had hopes of becoming the first club to win the treble of League Championship, FA Cup and European Cup. The record books show that United took the Championship, but Real Madrid ended their European Cup hopes in the semi-final and Villa ruined their chances of achieving the double by pipping them 2–1 at Wembley in a controversial Final. Villa, in fact, had extra reason for denying United Cup glory, for it was they who had been the last to win the double in the gaslight days of Victorian soccer some 60 years earlier.

Manchester United had defeated the previous year's finalists, Birmingham City, in the semi-final, and though Villa were glad that their neighbours were out of it, they felt the need to uphold the honour of Birmingham by succeeding in the Final. Villa had already put out another neighbour (West Brom) in their semi-final, and having been a bit lucky to do so over two matches against a very lively Albion team, some Villa fans felt that this might well be their year. Jimmy Dugdale was something of a latter-day Johnny Reynolds, who had seen off his old Albion clubmates, and, having collected a winners' medal with Albion in 1954, was looking forward to another Cup success! But he was the only Villa player to have known any kind of trophy success before – even long-serving Johnny Dixon had never been so close. The last time a Villa team had got so far as even to a semi-final was just before World War Two, several years before Dixon signed on.

One surprise, however, for Villa fans in the Final was the omission of centre-forward Derek Pace in favour of Billy Myerscough, who had suddenly appeared for the first team (and scored) in the semi-final replay against Albion. But the centre-forward spot was, in truth, a main weakness in the Villa team, and neither Pace nor Myerscough remained with Villa for long. Gerry Hitchens was signed in the winter of 1957 after Pace had been sold, and Myerscough held on for a while longer. For Pace, his omission (in the days before match substitutions) must have stung hard, for he was always a thorn against Villa in subsequent matches against his old club.

Villa's wing-half Stan Crowther was not to know that he would be back at Wembley the following year, but this time in the colours of Manchester United, as he was signed by the Manchester club after their tragic plane-crash at Munich in which several of the team lost their lives. Others were not able to play again. Many independent observers were therefore going to be watching the Busby Babes for the last time in this 1957 Wembley encounter.

The sixth-minute collision between United goalkeeper Ray Wood and Villa's McParland has evoked much discussion. Suffice to say, the referee, Frank Coultas from Hull, penalised the Villa player for the challenge.

Afterwards Coultas was quoted as saying: 'It was not a malicious foul. McParland did not try to harm Wood. He was just a bit too robust, as they call it, just a bit too enthusiastic in playing the traditional British game of getting stuck in.'

It was indeed bad luck for United, as Wood was stretchered off with a fractured cheekbone. Blanchflower donned Wood's jersey, Duncan Edwards switched to centre-half and Billy Whelan slotted in at left-half.

In the 10 minutes immediately after that clash it was clear-cut conflict between United's skill and strength, and Villa's violent tackling, causing one observer to remark: 'It will be a six-a-side contest at this rate, with players carried off and others sent off'. But common sense prevailed; United battled on, Villa played football as their fans knew they could, and eventually the Final became a much brighter and more entertaining contest. Despite their handicap, it must be said that United dominated the first 20 minutes.

Villa picked themselves up and pressed forward towards the interval. United again took control at the start of the second half but Villa gradually wore them down, and it was not long before McParland grabbed the first goal, a header from Dixon's cross which gave Blanchflower no chance at all. Five minutes later Billy Myerscough rattled the United crossbar, the ball came back into play and there was McParland, perfectly positioned to ram in number two. Wood came back into the action, only to trudge along the touchline, but he had to be marked, and this allowed United that little extra space which resulted in them pulling a goal back, via Tommy Taylor's head, with eight minutes to go. Wood went back into goal and United pushed up in search of an equaliser. Villa held on to win the Cup for the first time in 37 years, and a proud Johnny Dixon showed it off to the travelling supporters.

MATCH REPORT

WEMBLEY - SATURDAY 4 MAY
ASTON VILLA 2 MANCHESTER UNITED 1

Aston Villa: Simms, Lynn, Aldis, Crowther, Dugdale, Saward, Smith, Sewell, Myerscough, Dixon, McParland.

Manchester United: Wood, Foulkes, Byrne, Colman, Blanchflower, Edwards, Berry, Whelan, Taylor, Charlton, Pegg.

Scorers: Villa: McParland (2), United: Taylor.

Referee: F. Coultas.

Attendance: 100,000.

There is little or no doubt with the neutrals that the injury suffered by Ray Wood, the Manchester goalkeeper, within the first 10 minutes after a collision with Peter McParland had a dramatic effect on the outcome of the match. The reduction to 10 men meant that the lads from Old Trafford were forced to defend more than would have been expected, and this handed the initiative to the Villa. Edwards moved to centre-half when Jackie Blanchflower replaced Wood between the sticks and Edwards, together with the skipper, Roger Byrne, did everything they could to protect their stand-in 'keeper. Blanchflower had little difficulty as he settled into his new role as Villa were restricted to long-range efforts.

It was surprising that although Wood returned to make himself a nuisance on the wing it was the Reds who were in charge as the second 45 minutes started. On 68 minutes United's rugged and uncompromising resistance was finally overcome when Les Smith got the ball to Dixon, whose centre into the penalty box was met by the head of McParland. 1–0 to the Villa. Within five minutes the game was over when McParland scored his second on 73 minutes, latching onto the rebound when Dixon's shot hit the United crossbar. As League Champions, the Reds would not lie down, and although it did not affect the result they were seemingly more dangerous after going two goals down than at any other period of the 90 minutes. Regrettably for them, the only reward was with seven minutes remaining when Taylor headed home from Edwards' corner.

Jack recalls: The Wembley turf was from Cumberland so I felt very at home gliding over the 'green, green grass of home', although very early on I was aware of the task in front of me as I was being marked by Duncan Edwards in more ways than one! We later played Manchester United in the Charity Shield game that was the traditional season opener between the League Champions and the FA Cup winners. The game was staged at Maine Road Manchester and on this occasion Duncan 'did me', leaving me with a very bad ankle injury. As I lay on the ground in pain, he said 'That's for Wembley'.

Duncan Edwards, who died on 21 February 1958, two weeks after he and his Manchester United teammates were in a tragic plane crash in Munich, was widely expected to become one of the greatest players of all time. He was just 21 when he died, with a great future, both professional and

Give you a lift? Jack as a boy.

Kells Centre, 1944–45. Jack is seated on the ground in the front row, second from left.

Sewells and Buchanans. Jack is holding the ball.

The Kells crowd and Jack with the Cumberland Cup.

Being carried shoulder high after we had beaten the Army XI in the Cumberland Cup Final.

Football League Division Three
South champions medal 1949–50.

In action for Notts County, *c.*1949.

Notts County *c.*1944. Jack is in the front row, second from right.

Jack was best man at Tommy Lawton's wedding to Gaye. Tommy's mum is on the right.

Tommy Lawton and the lads wishing Jack well on his record transfer.

Notts County, champions of Division Three South. Jack is seated third row, fourth from left.

Division Two champions' medal.

Sheffield Wednesday, c.1952. Jack is on the front row, second from left.

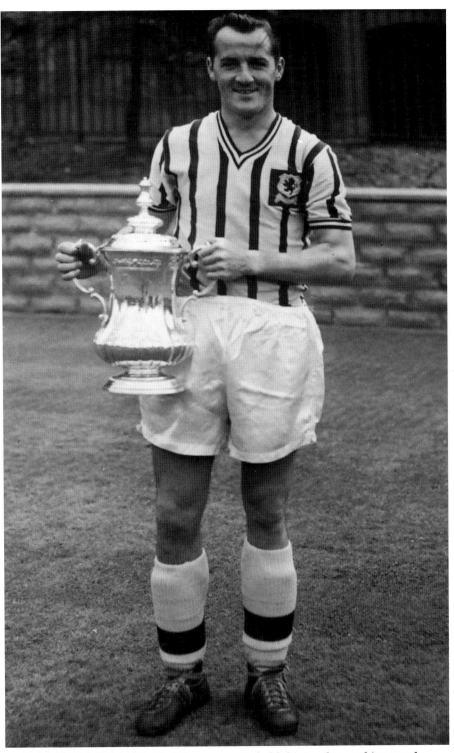

Jack with the FA Cup, won with Villa in 1957. To hold this trophy was his second ambition after playing for England.

Jack and Barbara married in December 1957.

Stan Lynn kisses the bride while Houghton and McParland look on.

Jack signs for Aston Villa.

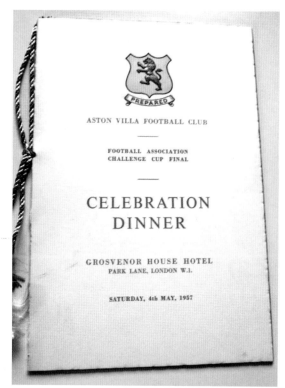

1957 Celebration Dinner Programme.

Cup-winners' medal.

Coming home after victory in the FA Cup Final.

A cup of tea with the skipper, Johnny Dixon, at the hotel on FA Cup Final day, 1957.

Eric Houghton's gift.

FA Cup line up.

Happy or what?

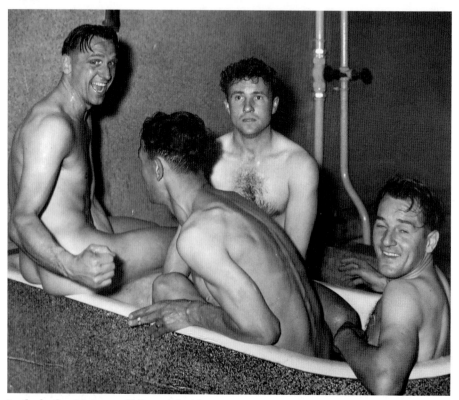

In the bath with Lynn, Aldis and Smith.

personal, ahead of him. Not only was he due to marry his girlfriend, he was already England's youngest 20th-century player, with an incredible 18 caps to his name.

Edwards was born on 1 October 1936 in Dudley in the West Midlands. His talents were brought to the attention of Manchester United by England Schoolboy coach Joe Mercer (that man gets everywhere!) when he was just 14. It took their scout 10 minutes to decide the club should sign him. They kept tabs on him for the next two years and signed him the day he turned 16.

Within a year he had become the youngest player to play in the First Division and quickly established himself as a key player in the team of prodigious talent known as the 'Busby Babes', a group of players brought through the United Youth team by Matt Busby and his assistant Jimmy Murphy.

The *Birmingham Sports Argus* carried the following article penned by local football reporter, Eric Woodward:

I will never forget this match as long as I live. I will never forget this Villa triumph for the personal battle fought on the sun-soaked Wembley turf by Peter McParland, scorer of the two goals which brought Villa the Cup again after 33 years. He battled against bitter barracking from United fans after colliding with 'keeper Ray Wood early on, and – like a true Villa man – kept battling right on until the end.

This Final had everything – thrills, drama, a fair ration of good football and a tense finish. I could go on. But it is sufficient to say that Villa, every man jack of them, gave everything they had – and it was too much for United.

Unquestionably Wood's injury marred what otherwise would have been a classic clash. I know Villa, like me, would rather have won against 11 fit men. Yet that's how it goes and United were the first to congratulate Villa – superb sportsmanship.

And to the obvious question, although it is being wise after the event. I insist that the Villa today would have beaten United at full strength. If ever a side deserved to win the Cup after battling against the odds all through the season, then Villa are the team. Thanks, boys, for the memory.

A six-minute shadow covered the first half. For it was then that Wood was hurt. Picture the scene. A superb Sewell cross was pin-pointed for McParland's head. It was a similar set-up to the first goal Villa's outside-left scored in the Molineux semi-final against West Bromwich Albion. But this time Peter did not connect properly and Wood cleared easily. The United 'keeper was holding the ball when McParland hurtled in and crashed against him. A foul? Unquestionably. Peter simply did not hit him squarely. But with deliberate intent to cripple? Most certainly not. McParland's enthusiasm upset his accuracy and instead of meeting Wood's shoulders he went across him. Consequently Wood was away 27 minutes before coming back at outside-right, but it was a great tragedy the accident ever happened, because to the vast majority of the crowd it took away the edge from some very fine football that Villa served up – good enough to grace any Wembley occasion. But the cheers were for gallant United, for deputy 'keeper Jackie Blanchflower's courageous show – and the boos were reserved for Villa as they went in at the break. Yet, if Villa had shown anything like the zip and accuracy around the box which they did in midfield, they would surely have been in a clear lead when they went off at the break. United were carried along on a wave of sympathy. In fact, it was shown very clearly that for much of the match Villa were playing 86,000 of the 100,000 crowd too.

McParland was booed every time he touched the ball – a bitter, senseless action – but he battled away gamely and was always dangerous in the air. And though United fought superbly to have an equal share of the second half, it was Villa who went nearest to scoring.

McParland soared up sweetly to head a Les Smith cross against the post, and Billy Myerscough blazed away a glorious chance on the other penalty spot. But how the faithful Villa 14,000 roared when a header from Villa's outside-left put Villa ahead and then slammed in a second.

It was indicative of Manchester United's incredible dominance in English football in 1957 that they got to Wembley without having to endure a replay. Their journey began with a surprisingly difficult away trip to Hartlepool United, whom they overcame, winning with the odd goal in seven, and in round four they destroyed Wrexham 5–0 at Wrexham. In the fifth round a single goal sent Everton out of the competition to leave the season's giant-killers Bournemouth & Boscombe United awaiting them in the quarter-final. They squeezed past 2–1 and dismissed Birmingham City, one of the previous season's finalists, 2–0 at Villa Park.

Jack remembers: Once we had got to the FA Cup semi-final stage of the 1957 tournament together with West Bromwich Albion and Birmingham City, in a unique event for the West Midlands clubs, the local football journalist, Charles Harrold, ran a series of Question and Answer articles with me for the local paper:

Question 1: *'Are Aston Villa through to the semi-final of the FA Cup because they are the current masters of mud?'*

Answer: The mud has had an influence, but let's be clear. We have not got there only because of the mud. We have not just slogged our way to the semi-final. We have played good football, too, when we have been able to. From the start of the season we have trained to be super fit; there is no fitter team than Villa. That has brought us through when conditions have been terrible – that and the fact that we have played straight-forward football that wins matches in the mud. If all grounds had been good I still think we should have got through, although it might have been more of a struggle. Conditions at Middlesbrough and Burnley were good. The Middlesbrough pitch was the best I have played on this year – and we played our best football in the Cup.

Question 2: *'When I have seen you play, physical strength and power seem to have been the major factor. Is this so?'*

Answer: That's probably because you have only seen us on heavy grounds in the Cup when physical fitness has been the deciding factor. It was certainly true against Bristol City, who gave us our hardest match. But we won in the end because we stayed the distance better than they did. We are nearly all big fellows and when big men are super-fit they are bound to look physically dominant, particularly in the tackle. You have got to be able to tackle well and win the ball often to do any good in the Cup.

Question 3: *'I suppose it is because of so much tackling that it is said you stop other people playing football?'*

Answer: And so we do – because we keep on taking the ball from them by good, honest tackling. And the less your opponents see of the ball the less football they can play. That means your side must have more of the ball but they must be able to do something with it to make progress. Out of this I think you can find the maxim for Cup success – first and foremost you must have the power and determination to get the ball and then make a show when you have got it. If you are a hard side with a fair amount of football then you can go all the way. It does not apply so much in the League because there is less tackling.

Question 4: *'You talk of strength and hardness in the tackle. Hasn't that led to the suggestion that you are a robust strong-arm side?'*

Answer: I can't deny that strongly enough. The lads have been riled by these suggestions from people who don't understand what they are saying. Certainly we go in hard and we go in quickly, and when a strong man knocks a little fellow off the ball it may look rough, but it is a long way from being anything like dirty. I dismiss it as a lot of silly talk. When it is 50–50 between two players in a tackle often the weaker player loses balance and goes down. You can't play if you can't get the ball, and we don't mean to lose sight of that. But to say we get it by rough tactics is ridiculous. I regard crude, wild tackling as rough play and you don't see it from Villa. My idea of rough play is the man who comes in with his foot up – and there is certainly none of that. We have backs and halves who go in quickly and hard but they are football-minded. If they weren't, we forwards would have a bad time – but we are enjoying ourselves.

Because I think a lot of tackling gets misinterpreted these days I want to say this: opponents cannot expect to hold the ball and bring it to us or try and drag it past us in the sludge and expect to get away with it. That gives us the chance to go in and we go in hard with the one and only intention of playing the ball. The player about to be tackled tries to flick the ball away. Sometimes, a split-second after the ball has gone, the tackler, following through with the pace of his tackle, is carried into the opponent. I agree it is a foul but it cannot be regarded as dirty because the intention was to play the ball.

Question 5: *'It is difficult to identify a clear-cut method in Villa's attacking play. Do you work to a basic plan?'*

Answer: If you mean anything as clear as, say, the Revie Plan then the answer is 'No' because we have tried to avoid a stereotyped way of playing. But we do work to a basic method. During the season we have developed the straight-forward ball, getting away more and more from the short square-passing. We want the ball played from behind as quickly as possible and straight into the attack, and we aim to get the wingers into position to enable them to cross as fast as they can into the penalty area to our men going forward with defenders still running back into position. We believe in one pass of 25 yards rather than two of 10 yards. The longer the pass the greater the chance of error, but the more effective it is when it clicks. We have analysed the things that each of us can do best. We have assessed ourselves as a team and we concentrate on a method that enables each man to do what he can most easily do, most often.

Question 6: *'They said you were a team without a chance when you reached the Final. Since then your record of five wins, two draws and three defeats, and with reserves in nearly every game, has made people notice. The greatest improvement has been in attack, with 19 goals for and 11 against in those 10 games. Have you developed a new attacking method since the semi-final?'*

Answer: I told you we weren't going to let Wembley worry us, and it hasn't. In fact, it has been very much the other way. There is nothing new in our forward play. We have had a pattern of going-on all season, but it has not been so evident because of two things. It is a variable system and therefore not so marked as some. We don't rely on one man to do one job. We work a moving centre-forward, but that doesn't mean only one other man, say Johnny Dixon, can go through the middle. The score sheet shows how the wingers – who have scored more goals than any Villa wing pair since before the war – and Dixon and myself have come through as spearheads. Secondly we are developing it more and more now, repeating the moves more often, and the very fact that it is coming on so well at this time is just what we wanted.

Question 7: *'So you feel that not only have you retained your edge for Wembley, but you will go there as a more effective attacking side?'*

Answer: I do indeed. I think we've come a long way since the semi-final. We're not accustomed to dry conditions and we have reached such a peak of confidence that we are trying things more often than are needed to make the attack pattern click. I, particularly, can feel the difference. From my point of view it is easier to play. The idea of how we want to play has 'bedded in' as it were. Men are wanting the ball and are easier to find because they know better what to do. I can look up now and see a man going straight away. That is the difference.

Question 8: *'In the semi-final the team seemed to be tense and your football suffered as a result. Isn't it possible that the Final atmosphere will have a similar effect?'*

Answer: I believe we have now established our attacking play to the extent that it will not be lost in the Final. It failed us to some extent in the semi-final, it is true, but only because it was not such a confirmed part of the side as it is now. And another thing, we're not playing relaxed football in the sense that we are taking it easy. The football looks relaxed because we are playing it now in the way we want to. The physical effort is still very much there, but is being applied differently. And I still believe we are going to win.

Question 9: *'I have never seen a team bound for the Cup Final play with such determination after the semi-final as Villa have done. How do you manage to put Wembley out of your mind?'*

Answer: In one sense it is very much in our minds. Not a day goes by when we are not concerned with such things as personal appearances, advertising or our souvenir booklet. But it is true that for 90 minutes in every game we forget Wembley. We are proud of what we have achieved this season. We've built up a record – one defeat in the last 17 games is part of it – and a big reputation. We don't want to lose face if we can help it. We have enough pride in ourselves not to allow people to toy with us and make us look silly. That would happen soon enough if we didn't try. Another thing: in 12 months we have known the difference between winning and losing runs. We know what winning, or at least not losing, does to a team's confidence, and the different atmosphere it creates in the dressing-room. We want to stay happy and full of confidence. There is no better way of ensuring that than by winning matches.

Question 10: *'Apparently that does not apply only to the Cup Final team. You beat Birmingham with five reserves in your side. How about that?'*

Answer: I'm quite sure it is a case of a new confidence having gone right through the club. The reserves are very conscious that we have reached the Final. They are determined not to let the club down.

Question 11: *'Your efforts since the semi-final have surprised many people, particularly as you were safe in the table. What do you say to that?'*

Answer: Being safe was not good enough for us. We believe we are as good as Manchester United, and the nearer we can finish to them in the League the better. Then people can't say, 'Here's United on top and Villa below halfway: what a difference!' We'll be a lot nearer to United by Wembley time.

Question 12: *'The worry of getting injured plagues so many teams on the way to Wembley. There seems little suggestion by Villa that players are concerned about getting hurt. What is your answer to this?'*

Answer: Before our first League game after the semi-final the boss called us together and reminded us that players having reached the Final often think too much about Wembley, and become obsessed with the idea of not getting hurt. 'It is when you start easing off and trying to avoid injury that you are most likely to get hurt,' he said. 'Now you're there, go out and enjoy your football and try to forget Wembley.' We appreciated the point because we knew he was right, and we tried to follow his advice.

Question 13: *'Isn't it surprising that you should have all weighed in 100 per cent with no exceptions?'*

Answer: The very fact that we have is typical of the great spirit at Villa Park. We are essentially a team with no individuals dominating the rest. In spite of playing matches every two days, as we have done recently, everyone has wanted to play. In fact, players with minor knocks have been forced to rest. Johnny Dixon, Les Smith and myself all had knocks after the Cardiff game. It was suggested that we should rest for the next match. None of us wanted to stand down, and in the end the boss had to make the decision. We have not played 'picnic' games since the semi-final, either. Four of the five matches have been against teams who have had particularly good reasons for wanting to win. We have failed only once – at Cardiff – and after that game we were disgusted with ourselves for losing because we knew we had tried to be exhibitionists. We thought Cardiff would be too easy after we had beaten them 4–1 a week before at Villa Park.

I remember we had a souvenir printed to raise some more money for the players' pool. (Author's note: *The Aston Villa Players' FA Cup Souvenir Handbook* was priced at 1s 6d. There was an advertisement which ran in the *Sports Argus*, together with the Co-op, promoting the *Handbook* with the offer: 'A real life Aston Villa player will hand you your book, think of that!')

Jack remembers: Our Final medals were made in Birmingham by Fattorini & Sons Limited at their Brentford works in Barr Street, and they were later inscribed on the back with the name of the player and the club. After the game we went to the Grosvenor House Hotel in Park Lane for our celebration dinner. It had been there since 1929 and is still frequented by royalty, celebrities and business leaders to this day. I bet they would be interested in seeing the programme I have for the Celebration Dinner.

The Aston Villa Football Club Celebration Dinner was a very formal affair and quite an unusual experience for the players. It was called a Celebration dinner as we did not know whether we would be celebrating a winners or a runners'-up medal.

The Celebration Dinner programme contains the following:

Page 1   The Officers of the Aston Villa Football Club

Page 2   Principal Records of the Aston Villa Football Club

Page 3   The Menu

Jack recalls: I remember a different drink was served with each of the courses; there were glasses everywhere, never mind knowing which fork and knife to use. There was sherry with the starter, which was a choice of either hors d'oeuvres or smoked salmon, but everything was in French so some of us did not know what we were ordering. We had wine with the fish course, and to accompany the main course, which was chicken with potatoes and peas (sounds better in French), we had Champagne with brandy or whisky. With the dessert and coffee we could have either beer or cider. There were a few of us who did not remember going to bed that night...

Page 4   The Toasts

'The Queen' was proposed by Sir Patrick Hanon (the club president), who also proposed a toast to the Football Association which was responded to by 'a representative of the FA'. The toast to 'the Aston Villa Football Club' was proposed by The Right Worshipful, The Lord Mayor of Birmingham, Alderman Ernest W. Apps JP, and was responded to by the club chairman, C.S. Buckley, and Mr J.T. Dixon, the captain. The final toast to 'the Guests' was proposed by Norman L. Smith, a Director of the club, with the response being given by Major H. Wilson Keys, the chairman of West Bromwich Albion Football Club.

Jack recalls: The speeches went on and on and we could not wait for the dancing and entertainment to begin – the cabaret was a conjurer called

George Braund, who reputedly had a stammer which disappeared once he was performing on stage. Very good he was too.

It was a fact that getting to a Wembley FA Cup Final gave teams experiences of the tournament, which meant that win or lose they would do well the following season. In 1955 Manchester City lost to Newcastle, only to win it in 1956 by beating Birmingham City, who got to the semi-finals in 1957 – and so it was for the Villa.

Aston Villa FA Cup 1958–59:

Round	Date	Venue	Opposition	Score	Scorers	Crowd
3	10/01/59	Home	Rotherham United	2–1	Sewell Hitchens	34,000
4	24/01/59	Away	Chelsea	2–1	Hitchens Myerscough	55,994
5	14/02/59	Away	Everton	4–1	Wylie (2) McParland, Hitchens	60,900
6	28/02/59	Home	Burnley	0–0		54,100
6 Replay	04/03/59	Away	Burnley	2–0	McParland (2)	39,023
Semi-final	14/03/59	Hillsborough	Nottingham Forest	0–1		*

(*Author's note: Although I have been unable to get an accurate attendance figure for the semi-final, the press reported ticket tout activity whereby Centre Stand seats with a face value of 25 shillings were being offered for £4 6 shillings, six-shilling Enclosure tickets for 30 shillings and Ground admission tickets of two-shillings and sixpence were fetching 10 shillings.)

Jack remembers: I was prevented from scoring a goal in the semi-final when Charlie Thomson, the Forest goalkeeper, 'nosed' a shot from me round the post for a corner. Somehow the ball bounced off his nose to safety. He could not have repeated it if he wanted to; it was just one of those things. I do not remember whether Charlie had a particularly big nose or not.

6

Chapter Six

MY ENGLAND APPRENTICESHIP

As a young footballer I had two great ambitions; to play for my country at full international level and to win the FA Cup. These were things aspired to by many but achieved by few, and to have been lucky enough to be one of those elite few gives me great pleasure. My appearance in the 1957 FA Cup is covered in Chapter Five, so this chapter covers my experiences in trying to achieve the first of my ambitions – to win a full England Cap. My first England cap was hard-earned and followed a long apprenticeship which began when I was at Notts County in 1949.

1949

FOOTBALL ASSOCIATION XI

Jack's first representative game was for the Football Association against Cambridge University in November 1949. It was reported in the press as:

The FA XI was a mixture of professional and amateur players, who won the game easily 3–1. Neate gave the FA an interval lead, Jackson equalised, but goals from the visitors by Goring and Sewell, who played a sound game, put the result beyond doubt.

ENGLAND B

Jack was selected as a reserve for the England B game against Holland on 22 February 1949 at Newcastle. He was one of five newcomers to the England set-up, the others being R. Dicks of Middlesbrough, R. Middleton of Chesterfield, Quested of Fulham and Walters of Tottenham Hotspur.

The team was: Middleton, Dicks, Swift (Sheffield Wednesday – captain), Quested, Hughes (Liverpool), Dickinson (Portsmouth), Walters, Mannion (Middlesbrough), J. Milburn (Newcastle United), R. Froggatt (Sheffield Wednesday), J. Froggatt (Portsmouth).

Reserves to travel: Fairbrother (Newcastle United), Sewell and S. Milburn (Chesterfield).

Trainer: Norman Smith (Newcastle United).

1950

FA TOUR OF CANADA AND UNITED STATES OF AMERICA

The travelling party was:

Player	Team
S. Hanson	Bolton Wanderers
F. Bowyer	Stoke City
R. Robinson	Middlesbrough
T.V. Ward	Derby County
R. Flewin	Portsmouth
H. Johnston	Blackpool
E. Russell	Wolverhampton Wanderers
C. Vaughan	Charlton Athletic
S. Matthews	Blackpool
J. SEWELL	NOTTS COUNTY
L. Medley	Tottenham Hotspur
N. Lofthouse	Bolton Wanderers
D. Wilshaw	Wolverhampton Wanderers
J. Hagan	Sheffield United
W. Ellerington	Southampton
J. Hancocks	Wolverhampton Wanderers
S. Milburn	Chesterfield
A. Mozley	Derby County
J. Taylor	Fulham
E. Wainwright	Everton
Trainer: T. Dawson	Grimsby Town

Of this party Ellerington, Hagan, Hancocks, Johnston, Matthews, Mozley and Ward had already gained full England caps, while Lofthouse, Medley, Taylor and Jack were capped at a later date. (Author's note: For completeness Reg Flewin had played for England in a wartime game.)

Jack recalls: It was a very successful tour on the field. We played 11 games in all, winning 10 and drawing the other.

Date	Location	Opposition	Score
20 May	Montreal	Montreal	7–0
24 May	Toronto	Ontario	4–1
27 May	Saskatoon	Saskatoon	19–1
30 May	Vancouver	Vancouver	4–4
1 June	Victoria	Victoria	3–2
3 June	Vancouver	British Colombia	7–1
7 June	Calgary	Alberta	9–0
14 June	Toronto	Manchester United	4–2
17 June	Windsor	Ontario	9–2
20 June	Randalls Island	USA	1–0
22 June	Montreal	Jonkopings Sodra IF (Sweden)	1–7

I scored a hat-trick when we beat Saskatoon All-Stars 19–1. Vaughan (Charlton), Hagan (Sheffield United) and Bowyer (Stoke City) each scored four goals each. One of the opposition All-Stars was our own Nat Lofthouse, who played for them along with Tim Ward as they only had nine players. As well as playing two other touring teams, Manchester United and Jonkopings Sodra, we also had a match on 10 June against the Blues and the Whites, which was won by the Blues 7–6, the teams being made up from both English and Canadian players. When we got back I played for the tourists against the World Cup XI at Stamford Bridge.

1951

FA TOUR OF THE UNITED STATES OF AMERICA AND AUSTRALIA

The travelling party for this tour was:

Player	Team
H. Bamford	Bristol Rovers
S. Bartram	Charlton Athletic
F. Broome	Notts County
T. Burgin	Sheffield United
I. Clarke	Portsmouth
R. Flewin	Portsmouth
J. Hagan	Sheffield United
G. Hurst	Charlton Athletic
L. Kieran	Tranmere Rovers
J. SEWELL	NOTTS COUNTY
B. Langton	Bolton Wanderers
F. Lock	Charlton Athletic
J. McCue	Stoke City
S. Owen	Luton Town
D. Parker	West Ham United
J. Shaw	Sheffield United
S. Milburn	Chesterfield
B. Smith	Birmingham City
H. Webster	Bolton Wanderers
Manager: D. Wiseman	

Of this party Broome, Hagan and Langton had already gained full England caps, while Owen and Jack were capped at a later date. (Author's Note: For completeness Reg Flewin had played for England in a wartime game, as had Sam Bartram.)

Jack recalls: This tour was even more successful than the previous one, as on this tour we played 21 games and won them all, conceding 14 goals but scoring 157! We had a management team of two. There was David Wiseman of Birmingham City, who was one of their directors and an FA Committee member, plus Frank Adams from Wycombe. On the way to Australia we beat an American team 4–0 in New York, and I scored as well as Langton and Smith, who got two.

Date	Location	Opposition	Score
9 May	New York	Americal Soccer League	4–0
16 May	Wollongong	South Coast	7–0
19 May	Sydney	New South Wales	8–1
22 May	Sydney	Metropolis	6–2
26 May	Sydney	Australia	4–1
30 May	Cessnock	Northern District	7–1
2 June	Newcastle	New South Wales	3–1
6 June	Victoria	Country XI	5–0
9 June	Melbourne	Victoria	7–0
11 June	Melbourne	Australia XI	6–1

16 June	Hobart	Tasmania	11–0
19 June	Launceston	Tasmania	17–0
23 June	Adelaide	Australia XI	13–1
30 June	Sydney	Australia	17–0
4 July	Brisbane	Queensland	7–1
7 July	Brisbane	Australia	4–1
11 July	Brisbane	Central Queensland	13–1
14 July	Sydney	Australia	6–1
18 July	Parramatta	Grancvilla District	5–2
21 July	Newcastle	Australia	5–0
22 July	Wollongong	New South Wales	2–0

Jack remembers: Our first real game was the one against New South Wales and there were over **40,000** people in the Sydney Showground (Author's note: 42,150 people paid £6,505) and we won **8–1** and I scored a hat-trick. I remember scoring all seven goals in the **7–0** defeat of Victoria at the Melbourne Cricket Ground. That was some effort!

Two of the games on the tour were designated 'Test Matches' and recognised by the hosts as full international games. In the 17–0 victory over Australia at the Sydney Cricket Ground Jack set an Australian record with his six goals – the highest number of goals in an Australian international football match. 14,147 people came to watch, paying £2,323, to not only see Jack get his double hat-trick, but also to see Clarke score four, Hagan three, Hurst three and Frank Broome's single.

FOOTBALL LEAGUE

Jack played for the English Football League on four occasions and was a reserve for one other match:

Date	Opposition	Venue
31 October 1951	Scottish League	Sheffield
24 September 1952	The Irish League	Wolverhampton
17 March 1953	League of Ireland – Reserve	Dublin
10 February 1954	League of Ireland	Manchester
28 April 1954	Scottish League	Chelsea

Jack's final game for the Football League side came a month before his final game for the full England side, which was the 7–1 defeat by Hungary in Budapest. Of the Football League side that played on that April night Gil Merrick, Billy Wright, Syd Owen, Peter Harris, Bedford Jezzard and Jack made that fateful trip to eastern Europe. For the record books:

FOOTBALL LEAGUE 4 SCOTTISH LEAGUE 0
STAMFORD BRIDGE

> ### TEAMS:
> Football League: Merrick (Birmingham), Ball (Bolton), Williams (Chelsea), Wright (Wolves), Owen (Luton), Bell (Bolton), Harris (Portsmouth), Sewell, Jezzard (Fulham), Haynes (Fulham), Mullen (Wolves).

> **Scottish League:** Martin (Aberdeen), Lapsley (St Mirren), Bunning (Queen of the South), Evans (Celtic), Stein (Celtic), Combe (Hibernian), Leggatt (Aberdeen), McMillan (Airdrie), Bauld (Hearts), Fernie (Celtic), Ormond (Hibernian).

Scorers: Sewell, Jezzard (2) and Haynes

It was Jack's performance in Sheffield against the Scottish League that gained Jack full international recognition. The local paper reported his selections as follows:

So satisfied were the England selectors with the Football League team which defeated the Scottish League last month, that they have chosen this XI en bloc for the match against Ireland at Villa Park. This means that Jackie Sewell, of Sheffield Wednesday, Len Phillips of Portsmouth and Gil Merrick of Birmingham City get international caps for the first time. The team will do their pre-match training at Leamington Spa. The Birmingham Combination club, Lockheed, have placed their ground at the disposal of the national side. Sewell takes over from Thompson (Aston Villa), and he proved in the Football League side that he can make a fine partner for Tom Finney.

Chapter Seven

ENGLAND

As we discussed in Chapter Six, Jack served a decent apprenticeship with various representative sides before being recognised by the England selectors; however, he ultimately achieved his ambition and played for his native country on six occasions. In this chapter I record his four matches for England, and the final two against Hungary are reported in Chapter Eight.

GAME ONE

ENGLAND 2 NORTHERN IRELAND 0

WEDNESDAY 14 NOVEMBER 1951

VILLA PARK, BIRMINGHAM

HOME INTERNATIONAL CHAMPIONSHIP

Manager: Walter Winterbottom.

Referee: Mervyn Griffiths (Wales).

Attendance: 57,889.

Scorers: Lofthouse 40 minutes, 83 minutes.

TEAMS:

England: Gil Merrick, Alf Ramsey, Lionel Smith, Billy Wright (Captain), Malcolm Barrass, Jimmy Dickinson, Tom Finney, Jackie Sewell, Nat Lofthouse, Len Phillips, Les Medley.

Northern Ireland: Norman Uprichard, Len Graham, Alf McMichael, Billy Dickson, Jack Vernon, Frank McCourt, Billy Bingham, Billy Smyth, Eddie McMorran, Jimmy McIlroy and John McKenna.

Jackie was not alone making his international debut against Northern Ireland, as that honour was also shared by Gil Merrick and Len Phillips. In this game Nat Lofthouse scored the 800th goal by England with his second-half strike.

The selectors experimented by giving inside-forwards Jackie Sewell and Len Phillips their first caps either side of Nat Lofthouse, who scored a goal in each half. Birmingham City goalkeeper Gil Merrick made the short journey to Villa Park for his first of 23 caps. He kept a clean sheet, but he was lucky in the second half when a screaming 25-yard shot from Barnsley forward Eddie McMorran crashed against the crossbar. Skipper Billy Wright gave a vintage performance and was the boss both of the defence and the midfield. His tackles were panther-like in their speed, and then he always found a teammate with a well-judged pass. Lofthouse scored both goals.

When Jack was picked to play for England a testimonial fund was immediately formed by the people of Kells to raise £100. Jack attended a function at the Kells British Legion Club, which he described as one of the most nerve-racking experiences of his life, as his football achievements were recognised by the very people who had given him his first taste of football success. In recognition of his success his was presented with a bureau of cutlery and a silver cigarette box. The testimonial fund committee comprised of:

J.W. Sinclair – Community Centre Warden was appointed Chairman.
J. Taylor – British Legion Secretary was appointed as Treasurer.
J.C. Evans – Town Councillor was appointed as Secretary.

The fund, restricted to Kells, received shillings, sixpences and so forth and soon £108 was raised. The biggest individual amounts were £22 from the proceeds of a dance in the Welfare Centre and £5 from the directors of the Whitehaven Rugby League Club. In addition to the cutlery and the cigarette box there was an illuminated address, the work of Mr L.S. Rockey, art master at Cleator School.

Presiding, Mr Sinclair spoke for the crowded gathering and all sports followers in Whitehaven when he said: 'We are extremely proud to have amongst us as one of our own kith and kin, a Kells lad who has gained fame in one of the greatest sports in the world.' Mr Sinclair said that quite probably Jack had been present at more illustrious gatherings, but nowhere would he find people more sincere. One thing about Jack was that he never failed to come home for his holidays. He loved his home and never forgot it, unlike many who gained fame and had a tendency to lose sight of their beginnings.

Mr Evans, handing over the gifts, said that while they were extremely proud of Jack's achievements they all hoped that the highest honour was yet to come next season – that of playing for England against Scotland at

Hampden Park. If that happened then all Kells would be up there shouting 'Up Kells!'

Mr W. Graham, a Legion official, thanked all who had made the presentation possible. Jack Sewell's was a household name the world over, and he assured him that he had the heartfelt wishes of the people of Kells for his future success.

Jack, who had been sitting with his mother and father, on rising to accept the gifts, said the last time he had felt so nervous was when he was signed by Sheffield Wednesday for £35,000. He was very proud that he came from Kells and he always knew when someone from Kells was watching him play. Even in a crowd of 54,000 he had often heard a lone voice shouting 'Come on Kells!'. It was not easy to rise to the top in football. 'You have to stick in and do your best and a fighting spirit is the best policy,' he added.

Jack, a most unassuming young man, said that some people might think that he had become big-headed, but he assured them that this would never happen. If, by chance, he walked past anyone it was perhaps that he had forgotten their faces through time.

Mr E.D. Smith, secretary of the Cumberland Football Association and a director of Workington Association Football Club, said that to him Jack Sewell was one of the ideal lads in football. He had started young and had taken heed of what that other Jack Sewell (his uncle) had told him. He and his other footballing relations had given young Jack the incentive and encouragement to become England's most costly player and almost England's best player. He would have liked to see the presentation in a bigger hall so that youths and boys could have attended. In that area were probably some of the best players yet to come, and he was rather surprised that the people of Kells were not giving their young players a chance to play soccer by failing to provide them with a ground. 'If you don't give them a chance, where are the other Jack Sewells to come from?'

Jack, he continued, was the finest example, along with Stanley Matthews, of having deserved the highest honour in the game. As for the future, Mr Smith said Jack was still young and he fully expected him eventually to play for England against Scotland.

Finally, Mr Sinclair thanked Mr Evans, the prime mover in the fund, and the British Legion. He added that he would like to correct the impression that the Welfare Centre did not wish to encourage young footballers. He hoped that next season there would be a Kells soccer team.

(Author's note: Jack never achieved the honour of playing for England against Scotland at Hampden Park.)

GAME TWO

AUSTRIA 2 ENGLAND 3
SUNDAY 25 MAY 1952
PRATER STADIUM, VIENNA
FRIENDLY

Manager: Walter Winterbottom.
Referee: Carpani (Italy).
Attendance: 64,000.
Scorers: Lofthouse 25 minutes, Huber 27 minutes, Jackie Sewell 28 minutes, Dienst 42 minutes, Lofthouse 83 minutes.

> **TEAMS:**
>
> **England:** Gil Merrick, Alf Ramsey, Bill Eckersley, Billy Wright (Captain), Jack Froggatt, Jimmy Dickinson, Tom Finney, Jackie Sewell, Nat Lofthouse, Eddie Baily, Les Medley.
>
> **Austria:** Josef Musil, Rudolf Rockl, Ernst Happl, Walter Schleger, Ernst Ocwirk (Captain), Theodor Brinek, Ernst Melchior, Gerhard Hanappl, Robert Dienst, Adolf Huber, Walter Haummer.

Jack recalls: Undoubtedly my most memorable game for England was against Austria when we were on a European Tour. That day we played together in such a way that it was never repeated in my experience, spurred on by thousands of members of the British Forces, it got the hairs on the back of your neck to rise with patriotism.

It was the first time we played in red shirts, and because of the quality of our performance that day, the selectors allowed us to keep our kit. It was also memorable for the fact that I scored my first international goal.

This was the match that earned Nat Lofthouse the nickname 'the Lion of Vienna'. Eight minutes from the end, with the game deadlocked at 2–2, Tom Finney collected a long throw from Gil Merrick and released a pass that sent Lofty clear just inside the Austrian half. He galloped 45 yards with a pack of defenders snapping at his heels, and collided with oncoming goalkeeper Musil as he released a shot. He was flat-out unconscious and did not see the ball roll over the goalline for the winning goal. The Bolton hero was carried off on a stretcher, but, still dazed, returned for the final five minutes. He struck a shot against a post in the closing moments.

England's counter-attacking tactics had worked to perfection. They took the lead in the 21st minute after soaking up non-stop pressure from the Austrians, who were rated the number-one team in Europe. A penetrating pass by Eddie Baily opened the heart of the Austrian defence and Lofthouse finished off the move with a left-foot volley deep into the net.

The cheers of the squads of British soldiers in the 65,500 crowd were still filling the Prater Stadium when Jack Froggatt conceded a penalty from which Huber side-footed an equaliser. The Portsmouth centre-half quickly made amends with a pass that put Jackie Sewell through to score after he had wrong-footed the Austrian defenders with two exaggerated dummies. Austria pulled level again just before half-time through centre-forward Dienst, who shrugged off Billy Wright's challenge before powering the ball past goalkeeper Gil Merrick. Then came the storybook climax from Lofthouse. The triumphant England players were carried back to their dressing-room on the shoulders of cheering Tommies, who had come from their posts in Germany in their thousands.

'MATCH OF THE CENTURY'
BY ALF RAMSEY

Judging by some of the newspapers we read, there was some disappointment with the performance of the England team against Italy. When the following day we departed for the old-world city of Siena, halfway between Florence and Rome, I did not feel so worried over the prospect of playing the Austrians as did some of the critics.

From Siena the whole England party moved up to Vienna on the Friday preceding the game. First we went by rail to Rome. After a short run around the Eternal City in a motor coach we had to board our plane for Vienna, for, as it proved to be, one of the greatest international soccer matches of all time.

I do not think any of us will ever forget the spectacle of Vienna ablaze with lights as it lay beneath the wings of our plane and the feeling when we landed to be the first England soccer team to go behind the 'Iron Curtain' – the airport was in the Russian sector, even if only a tiny bit inside Soviet-held territory!

On Saturday morning we put in some light training and in the afternoon visited the British Embassy, where a most excellent reception had been arranged. Behind all the pleasantries, however, I had a feeling that everyone, especially the servicemen present, were hoping we would give the Austrians a soccer lesson.

I never doubted that we would win. At Wembley Stadium, when the Austrians held us to a 2–2 draw, we learnt a great deal. No matter what anyone else may tell you, English professional footballers are not 'mugs' who just step on to a football field and hope for the best.

For weeks before the match in Vienna we had 'lived Austria'. Everything possible was done to make sure we had the low-down on our opponents as individuals and as a team. We became as familiar with their tactics as we were with our own.

When we took the field at the Prater Stadium, England – for the first time in years – found their opponents really hot favourites to beat them! The British Tommies gave us a real welcome, as we made our appearance. It did not take long for the Austrian crowd to get 'warmed up', however. Their champions, showing some delightful footwork, made ground so quickly that everyone at the Prater Stadium, with the exception of the England team, must have thought the Austrians were going to score a sack of goals. What everyone seemed to overlook was our system of 'retreating defence', which gave goalkeeper Gil Merrick the maximum cover and also seemed to put the ballet-dancing Austrians completely off their stroke when they approached our penalty area. It was all very nice for them to make ground with deft cross-passes, but when they reached our penalty area they found every player to whom they might pass the ball squarely covered.

The Prater Stadium crowd have a reputation for being one of the most one-sided in European soccer circles, but they seemed to excel themselves for our benefit. Evert time an Austrian was tackled there was a roar for a penalty. If we chested the ball down the roar for a spot-kick was repeated.

Then the Austrian fanatics were silenced. Twenty-seven minutes after the start, Jackie Sewell, who had been playing as an advanced inside forward, gave Nat Lofthouse a splendid pass, and before Musil knew what had happened the England centre-forward had flashed the ball into the Austrian goal. It was the first real shot we had tried during the match.

A minute after we had scored they had equalised, although it was a goal which left a nasty taste in our mouths. I was just behind Jack Froggatt our centre-half, when he made a tackle upon Dienst, Austria's centre-forward. Froggatt did not touch Dienst, but the Austrian leader threw himself full length, the crowd roared and referee Carpani, to my amazement, pointed to the penalty spot. As England players we did not, of course, protest. Huber made no mistake from the spot.

Inside a minute England had taken the lead once more when Jackie Sewell took a delightful pass from Lofthouse, sent two Austrian defenders going the wrong way with a splendid dummy and then planted the ball into the back of the Austrian net.

Just before half-time, Dienst equalised for Austria. Now the crowd at the Prater Stadium really did become a trifle – shall I say – nasty. Every time we went into a tackle they roared for a penalty, while the Austrian team, perhaps in their anxiety to score, conveniently forgot the rules. Some of their tactics were better suited to the rugby field, and one distinguished Austrian lost the respect of us all when he appeared to lift Jackie Sewell bodily into the air and then send our inside-right crashing to the ground heavily. I feared he was seriously injured when carried off the field for 'repairs' by trainer Jimmy Trotter. Fortunately for us, Sewell, a former miner, is as tough as granite and quickly recovered. We crossed over still holding them to a 2–2 draw.

Slowly but surely we got a grip upon the game and never relaxed. Try as they might, however, Austria could never regain the initiative. Sheer endeavour, and handing out some hard knocks, became their maxim. The old smoothness left the side. Instead of a sweetly-moving team they became a band of hard-working individuals, and as the minutes passed, so did England begin to 'click' in the manner expected of an international side. Yet, the conceding of a corner-kick played a major part in us scoring what proved to be the winning goal.

Nine minutes from the end, when Austria forced a corner-kick on the left, nearly the entire team packed into our penalty area. With the crowd roaring the Austrians on, things, I must admit, looked a little 'dickie' for England, but Merrick, towering above all others, leapt like a giant stag into the air as the ball was centred from the left wing, avoided a couple of Austrian forwards and heaved a wonderful pass up the centre of the field to Tom Finney, who had moved in from the right.

Finney flicked the ball onto Lofthouse, and before anyone quite realised what had happened he had ploughed his way like a tank down the middle of the field, which was wide open because of the over-enthusiasm of some goal-hungry defenders.

In the Austrian goal their 'keeper, Musil, began to jump up and down like a cat on hot bricks. To everyone it was obvious he was completely taken aback by this sudden crisis. One minute it appeared as if he were going to rush out and tackle Lofthouse then next he seemed to be glued to his goalline. And all the time the red-shirted Lofthouse, with fleet-footed Austrians beginning to gain upon him, kept on his way.

Then, like a frightened hare, Musil suddenly leapt from his goal. It was then Lofthouse showed his greatness, coolness and confidence. Ignoring the 13 stone of goalkeeper threatening to envelop him, he picked his spot in the Austrian goal – about 2ft inside the right-hand post – and put everything he possessed into a ripping right-foot drive. Then, as Musil and Nat went down in a flurry of arms and legs, the ball flew like a rocket into the back of the Austrian goal.

'I guess that was the longest 45 yards I've ever run', was the first comment of Lofthouse as his colleagues helped him to his feet.

Nat's effort had not been gained without a painful injury, and in a matter of seconds he was behind the goal for treatment to an injured knee. He returned to play on the left wing, and he then crashed in a superb drive which hit the foot of the post with the Austrian 'keeper beaten all ends up.

Now the superb fitness which trainer Jimmy Trotter had helped bring about showed itself. The Austrians were sent reeling back upon their heels, with a series of attacks which might easily have brought us more goals. I'd hazard the view, too, that if the match had continued for another 10 minutes we would have scored at least three times, for I have rarely seen any side so completely outplayed as were the Austrians.

Then followed a scene which can never have before happened to an England football team. With many Russians beaming, hundreds of English Tommies, members of the Forces of Occupation, swarmed on to the field and before the English players quite knew what had happened we were all lifted into the air, rested upon the shoulders of excited Tommies and carried in triumph to the dressing-room.

'We ain't half pleased mate,' said one excited soldier to me, 'because for months the local lads have been telling us what they're going to do to you. Well,' he grinned, 'you well and truly done 'em mate.'

Gil Merrick, England goalkeeper on 23 occasions, recalls:

It was 1952 and Austria were perceived as being the Champions of Europe – this was the days before the European Championship began and their captain had been crowned European Footballer of the Year. Both England and Austria were unbeaten that season, having held us to a draw some months before at Wembley, therefore the match in Vienna was looked upon as being the match to decide who was the best international side in Europe.

The crowd was swelled by the attendance of over 1,000 British servicemen who were given leave to attend the game. The atmosphere was fantastic. It was 2–2 with about six minutes to go when the Austrians won a corner on the right. I managed to catch it and cradle the ball to my chest, but as I did that, Dienst, the Austrian centre-forward slapped the ball hard with his hand in an attempt to get me to drop the ball. I held on but the referee did not see it. I turned away from the ruck of players, bounced the ball once and quickly took a view of the field. There was Nat Lofthouse and Tom Finney within two or three yards of each other near the centre circle. I hurled the ball 35 yards up to Finney, who crossed the ball first time to Nat Lofthouse. Nat ran 40 yards to score the winner and was from that day known as 'the Lion of Vienna'.

The Tommies went mad! I often think what would have happened if I hadn't been able to hold on to that ball and it had been knocked out of my hands. They would probably have scored and history would have been very different.

Nat Lofthouse – 'the Lion of Vienna' – was the last great champion of a dying breed: the traditional English centre-forward. The talismanic figurehead given the job of leading the line, taking more than his share of knocks and scoring most of the goals.

Over a period of eight years, the Bolton Wanderers forward scored 30 times in 33 internationals – and only Jimmy Greaves has been able to match that strike rate over a prolonged period.

Lofthouse was an old-style number nine, like Dixie Dean and Tommy Lawton before him. 'A battering ram,' as he once described himself modestly. Tom Finney was far more generous, listing his attributes as 'speed, fearlessness, a hard shot in either foot, good heading ability and a robust frame to stand up to all the physical stuff.'

His nickname was bestowed on him for his performance in scoring the winning goal in England's 3–2 win over Austria in Vienna in 1952 – a match billed as an unofficial Championship of Europe. Lofthouse was knocked unconscious briefly but insisted on returning to the action despite a knee injury. 'The courage Nat showed was typical of him,' Alf

Ramsey said. 'The way he insisted on coming back on lifted the heart of every Englishman in the stadium. It made us redouble our efforts to keep the Austrians out.'

His performance in the FA Cup Final of 1953 was another highlight: Lofthouse scored one goal, hit the post, harassed his opponents and was almost knocked unconscious. At the end of the game, he walked over and shook the hands of the victorious Blackpool players.

Such sportsmanship, allied to his loyalty to Bolton, his only club, added to his public appeal. Voted Footballer of the Year in 1953, Lofthouse was elated when his conduct on the field was praised as highly as his scoring prowess.

Five years later, Bolton were back at Wembley for an FA Cup Final against Manchester United. All 11 Wanderers players were local lads, and each of them had cost the club only a £10 signing-on fee. This time, Lofthouse scored twice, controversially bundling the ball into the net with a shoulder charge against Harry Gregg, the Manchester United goalkeeper, for one of his goals in a 2–0 victory.

Born and bred in Bolton, Lofthouse signed for Wanderers as a 14-year-old amateur in 1939, and he played his 503rd and last game for them 21 years later, with 285 goals to his credit.

The start of his League career was delayed by the outbreak of World War Two, the conflict that shaped him as a player. 'It toughened me up, physically and mentally,' Lofthouse recalled. Too young for military service, he worked in a coal mine, pushing tubs of coal, building his strength and fitness.

Lofthouse played his final game – against Birmingham City – in December 1960 following a long lay-off with a cruciate ligament injury.

Football was changing. As his career was coming to an end, so was the golden age of the English centre-forward. His generation had played a simpler game tactically, with the number nine as the 'pivot' of the attack. Len Shackleton put it this way: 'Billy Wright won the ball and passed it to me. I gave it to Stan Matthews who ran down the wing and centred for Nat Lofthouse, who scored.'

In Charles Buchan's *Football Monthly*, the great man wrote this article:

'THE EPIC OF ELEVEN GALLANT ENGLISHMEN'
CHARLES BUCHAN ON ENGLAND'S TOUR

British soldiers of the Dorsetshire Regiment scampered across the Stadium in Vienna and carried the England players shoulder-high to the dressing room after their glorious 3–2 victory over Austria. It was a terrific demonstration from young soldiers who had been continuously told that Austria were going to trounce the declining Englishmen. It was also the most gallant victory ever brought off by an England team on the Continent.

Everything, except the conditions – which were like an early April day with rain pouring down – was against them from the start. Referee's decisions, including a penalty-kick against Froggatt, dangerous kicking and body-checking that had to be seen to be believed, and the run of the ball, which went in Austria's favour, seemed to conspire against them. Yet they fought through, with two or three players hobbling about, to such a victory that in the end the Austrians were practically run off their feet.

It was a tremendous triumph for teamwork, and, in plain language, guts. Every member of the team pulled out the best that was in him.

I must first raise my hat to three gallant English gentlemen. First to Nat Lofthouse, a dynamic centre-forward who not only scored two goals, but, almost crippled from the effort which brought the winning goal 10 minutes from the end, nearly added two more through sheer courage. Before the game the Austrians labelled him 'The Tank'. After it they paid ample tribute to his skill and never-say-die spirit. His winning goal was an epic. Receiving the ball on the halfway line, he outstripped the tiring Austrian defenders. Approaching goal, he took the ball up to the Austrian goalkeeper, and as Musil dived despairingly at his feet, coolly steered the ball past him. Lofthouse got the full weight of the goalkeeper on his shin, but, though in pain, carried on. He told me: 'I would have left my leg at the halfway line rather than miss the chance'. It was typical of the lion-hearted Bolton centre-forward.

Jack Froggatt, the Portsmouth ironman, also put on a show almost beyond praise. He twisted his knee early in the game, and then, in the second half, got a painful knock on the thigh. Yet he never flinched. His tackling and command over the goalmouth area reminded me of the great 'old-timer' Alex Raisbeck.

Gil Merrick, of Birmingham, established himself as England's number-one goalkeeper. One save of his in the early stages was beyond belief. So sure was the 65,000 Austrian crowd that it was impossible for him to parry a shot from Dienst, they clamoured for a penalty-kick. They were positive that left-back Bill Eckersley had punched the ball out. Tom Finney, England's outside-right, who received particularly close attention from the Austrians, told me afterwards: 'Only those who played in it can realise how tough the game was.' Tom was another star in the gallant band who had the English element present roaring with excitement and admiration.

To the others, to inside-forwards, Eddie Baily and Jackie Sewell, scorer of the second goal, to outside-left Billy Elliot, who played his heart out, to captain Billy Wright, to Jimmy Dickinson, whose deadly tackling made the Austrians keep out of his way, to Alf Ramsey and Bill Eckersley, a sure shield in front of Merrick, hearty congratulations to all on a difficult job, nobly done.

GAME THREE

SWITZERLAND 0 ENGLAND 3
WEDNESDAY 28 MAY 1952
HARDTURM, ZURICH
FRIENDLY

Manager: Walter Winterbottom.

Referee: Louis Baert (Belgium).

Attendance: 33,000.

Scoreline: Sewell 13 minutes, Lofthouse 51 minutes, 87 minutes.

TEAMS:

England: Gil Merrick, Alf Ramsey, Bill Eckersley, Billy Wright (Captain), Jack Froggatt, Jimmy Dickinson, Ronnie Allen, Jackie Sewell, Nat Lofthouse, Eddie Baily, Tom Finney.

Switzerland: Thomas Preiss, Willy Kernan, Roger Bocquet, Hannes Schmidhauser, Olivier Eggiman, Willy Neukom, Robert Ballaman, Josef Hugi, Rene Bader, Lucien Pasteur, Jacques Fatton.

Billy Wright was credited with taking over the England caps record from Bob Crompton with this 43rd international appearance (although most record books give Crompton's old record as 41 caps). The Swiss were beaten by the same scoring combination that had won the match in Vienna three days earlier: Jackie Sewell one, Nat Lofthouse two. West Bromwich Albion's versatile forward Ronnie Allen won the first of his five caps, and gave a lively performance on the right wing.

The games against Austria and Switzerland were the last two games of a three-match tour of Europe. The first game was a 1–1 draw with Italy in Florence on 18 May 1952 in front of a crowd of 93,000. Broadis, who played in Jackie's inside-right position, scored for England, Amadel for Italy.

TOUR SUMMARY

18 May 1952 at Florence (Attendance 93,000), Italy 1 (Amadei) England 1 (Broadis).

25 May 1952 at Vienna (Attendance 65,000), Austria 2 (Huber (pen), Dienst) England 3 (Lofthouse (2), Sewell).

28 May 1952 at Zurich (Attendance 33,000), Switzerland 0 England 3 (Lofthouse (2), Sewell).

Goals: For 7 Against 3.
Scorers: Lofthouse 4, Sewell 2, Broadis 1.

GAME FOUR

NORTHERN IRELAND 2 ENGLAND 2
SATURDAY 4 OCTOBER 1952
WINDSOR PARK, BELFAST
HOME INTERNATIONAL CHAMPIONSHIP

Manager: Walter Winterbottom.
Referee: D. Gerrard (Scotland).
Attendance: 58,000.
Scoreline: Lofthouse 1 minute, Tully, Tully, Elliott 90 minutes.

TEAMS:

England: Gil Merrick, Alf Ramsey, Bill Eckersley, Billy Wright (Captain), Jack Froggatt, Jimmy Dickinson, Tom Finney, Jackie Sewell, Nat Lofthouse, Eddie Baily, Billy Elliott.

Northern Ireland: Norman Uprichard, Willie Cunningham, Alf McMichael, Danny Blanchflower, Billy Dickson, Frank McCourt, Billy Bingham, Seamus D'Arcy, Eddie McMorran, Jimmy McIlroy, Charlie Tully.

Nat Lofthouse scored (his 10th for England) in the first minute and Billy Elliott (his first for his country) in the last minute of a dramatic match. Sandwiched in-between was the magic of Celtic ball artist Charlie Tully, who scored twice for Ireland. He beat Merrick from 25 yards, and did it again with his specialist inswinging corner-kick after the Irish team had been reduced by injury to 10 men.

Northern Ireland, urged on by a record 60,000 Windsor Park crowd, had two young midfield partners called Danny Blanchflower and Jimmy McIlroy dictating the pace and the pattern of the match. They were on the verge of their first victory over England since 1927 when Elliott silenced the celebrating fans with an equalising header in the desperate closing moments. Billy Wright and Jimmy Dickinson were the match stars for England, steadying the ship with their cool defensive work when the Irish threatened to take a stranglehold on the game.

Team manager Walter Winterbottom was furious about the goal that Charlie Tully scored direct from a corner-kick. Charlie was famous for his in-swinging corners, and England had worked at cutting them out in training by placing Alf Ramsey on the near post and centre-half Jack Froggatt directly behind goalkeeper Gil Merrick. The corner from Tully he scored was curling towards Ramsey, who suddenly ducked under the ball. Gil reached out but only caught thin air as the ball swung into the net. Alf said later that he thought Gil had shouted 'mine', but it had apparently been one of the Irish forwards. The crowd went berserk when the ball hit the net. And no wonder – it was Northern Ireland's first international goal for 18 months!

Jack's England career spanned two years and 189 days.

Chapter Eight

HUNGARY

Prior to the first of the two games played with Hungary, which are recorded in this chapter, the England football team had been undefeated since 1901 by teams from outside the British Isles on home soil.

The invincible England side were defeated by superior technique and the Hungarians' desire to change the way the game was played. Up until the first game all teams had complied with the traditional system of marking and positional play. That was defined as: the right winger stayed wide and was marked by the left full-back, the centre-forward ploughed down the centre of the pitch and was marked by the centre-half, the inside-forwards were looked after by the wing-halves and the left winger stayed out on the left and was marked by the right full-back. That was the way the game was played, but no one told the Hungarians.

In a newspaper article on the morning of the Wembley match, J.G. Orange wrote:

'ENGLAND SHOULD BEAT HUNGARY'

This afternoon, at Wembley Stadium, England's footballers meet Hungary in an international match for the third time. Hungary beat us at Budapest in 1934 by 2–1, and two years later, at Highbury, England beat Hungary by 6–2, so today's game is in the nature of a decider.

It is interesting to recall our side against Hungary 17 years ago. It was: Tweedy (Grimsby), Male (Arsenal), Catlin (Sheffield United), Britton (Everton), Young (Huddersfield), Keen (Derby), Crooks (Derby), Bowden (Arsenal), Drake (Arsenal), Carter (Sunderland) and Brook (Manchester City).

Is our team of today inferior to that side? I do not think so. Indeed, I think our present team would beat the England side of 1936 as it was then in the matter of age and form. How then does this fear arise that England will be beaten today by Hungary? I do not share it, but the view is prevalent. I put it down largely to deep disappointment at the rather tame display put up by the England team against FIFA at Wembley five weeks ago, when a penalty goal by Ramsey in the closing seconds saved us.

I have listened to arguments that our conception of the game needs changing. I do not agree. The Continentals, including the Dynamos, play no better than the famous Scottish Wizards did at Wembley in 1928. They made the England team of that year look a much worse side than they were and much worse than any Continental side has ever done.

Where I believe we have been wrong in recent years is in not choosing the best inside-forwards available and in not making those selected work as inside-forwards.

141

The lack of co-operation or team work in this respect nearly cost England her record only five weeks ago. Then the inside-forwards stayed upfield and left gaps far too big for the wing-halves to take care of on their own. The upshot was that the FIFA insides had large spaces in which to work, made every possible use of them and made themselves look much better players than we could have permitted them to be.

From that match there is a lesson for today. Kocsis and Puskas, both master inside-forwards in their own realm, must not be permitted to roam at large. There must be an immediate challenge to them not only when they get the ball but before, when the ball is on the way to them. That first challenge will probably have to come from our own inside-forwards, leaving the wing-halves with a second chance. Our players need briefing on those lines before they take the field, and then it is up to Billy Wright, England's captain, to see that the briefing instructions are carried out on the field. The Hungarians are reputed to be exceedingly clever at inside-forward and it may take us all our time to check them. They are also fast and skilful on the wings, so there should be plenty of power in their attack. Yet a Continental friend who has seen Hungary's recent matches told me he would sooner have our forward line.

Hungary play the normal defensive game with Lorant as a strong stopper at centre-half. We should not have to worry much about his wanderings, as we had to with Ocwirk (Austria). The backs are powerful, swift into the tackle and strong kickers.

I am glad Ramsey is back in England's team. His cool presence means a great deal to the rest of the side, and even if he is a bit slow on the turn nowadays he often gets in quickly enough to prevent the left-winger doing any damage.

With Sewell and Ernest Taylor in the forward line we should be stronger than against FIFA. Every good back in the country seems to speak well of Sewell, while Taylor has a complete understanding with Stanley Matthews. But the pair must avoid any temptation to keep the ball tight on the right wing. Matthews, if he gets half-a-yard start, will be able to beat the quick tackle he may expect from Lantos. Mortensen's lively presence will mean that England will have a go for all the scoring chances and half-chances in the middle. He has still a great burst of speed and is a most persevering player. As for Robb, who gets his first full international cap (a distinction he shares with Ernest Taylor today), if he has got over his early-season idea of running the ball to the corner flag he will probably make good. But I should have been more confident of our winning had Finney or Mullen or Metcalfe or even Blunstone been at outside-left.

I plump for England to win 3–1. I am sure that on our own soil we can beat the Hungarians, and we shall win comfortably if our players think of the team more than they think of themselves.

GAME FIVE

ENGLAND 3 HUNGARY 6
WEDNESDAY 25 NOVEMBER 1953
WEMBLEY STADIUM, LONDON
FRIENDLY

Manager: Walter Winterbottom.
Referee: Leo Horn (Holland).
Attendance: 100,000.

Scoreline: Hidegkuti 1 minute, Sewell 13 minutes, Hidegkuti 20 minutes, Puskas 24 minutes, Puskas 27 minutes, Mortensen 38 minutes, Bozsik 50 minutes, Hidegkuti 53 minutes, Ramsey (penalty) 57 minutes.

TEAMS:

England: Gil Merrick, Alf Ramsey, Bill Eckersley, Billy Wright (Captain), Harry Johnston, Jimmy Dickinson, Stan Matthews, Ernie Taylor, Stan Mortensen, Jackie Sewell, George Robb.

Hungary: Gyula Grosics (Captain), Jeno Buzanszky, Mihaly Lantos, Joszef Bozsik, Gyula Lorant, Joszef Zakarias, Laszlo Budai, Sandor Kocsis, Nandor Hidegkuti, Ferenc Puskas, Zoltan Czibor.

Substitute for Grosics after 78 minutes Sandor Geller.

This was England's first defeat by foreign opponents on home territory, and the match that changed the face of English football. The Hungarians, Olympic champions and on a run of 29 successive matches without defeat, played to a flexible 4-2-4 formation and made England's 2-3-5 pattern seem about as outdated as a hansom cab on a motorway. Nandor Hidegkuti, a deep-lying centre-forward, nipped in for a hat-trick as two-goal Ferenc Puskas pulled the defence inside out. England were flattered by the 6–3 scoreline. Alf Ramsey, Bill Eckersley, Harry Johnston, Ernie Taylor, Stan Mortensen and George Robb never played for England again. Taylor and Robb were making their debuts.

Hungary had given just a taste of what was to come in the first minute when Hidegkuti collected a through ball from Puskas, deceived centre-half

Johnston with a distracting dummy and then fired the ball high into the net from 20 yards. Gil Merrick was left flapping at mid-air. Moments after Sewell had equalised in the 15th minute England were flattened by a 13-minute burst of Magyar magic. Two goals from the purist Puskas and another from the elusive Hidegkuti made it England 1, Hungary 4.

The 100,000 Wembley spectators could not believe their eyes. Stan Mortensen pulled it back to 4–2 by half-time, but any hope England had of getting back into the game died within 10 minutes of the second half. First the cultured Jozef Bozsik scored with a rising drive, then Hidegkuti completed his hurricane hat-trick when he put the finishing touch to a dazzling succession of passes that ripped the England defence apart. Alf Ramsey scored a late penalty after his Tottenham teammate George Robb, a schoolmaster, was pulled down by goalkeeper Grosics. The final scoreline could easily have read 10–3 to the Hungarians. Billy Wright had never been given such a chasing in all his life as the one he got from Ferenc Puskas.

Jackie recalls: I think one of the main reasons we came such a cropper against the Hungarians is that the selection committee were impressed with Blackpool winning the FA Cup in the May, when they beat Bolton 4–3. This became known as the 'Matthews Final', hence the changes in the starting line up. From the previous game only Merrick, Ramsey, Eckersley and Wright kept their places and their positions. I was switched to inside-left and Tom Finney was dropped for Stan Matthews, and I moved over – taking Eddie Baily's place – so that Ernie Taylor could come in on the right. Nat Lofthouse was replaced by Stan Mortensen, who had scored a Wembley hat-trick, and Jack Froggatt's centre-half role went to Harry Johnston, Blackpool's Cup-winning captain. Just to finalise the changes George Robb came in for Billy Elliott. It was a huge mistake to make so many changes against a team that were the Olympic Champions and had a very consistent team selection.

GAME SIX

HUNGARY 7 ENGLAND 1
SUNDAY 23 MAY 1954
NEPSTADION, BUDAPEST
FRIENDLY

Manager: Walter Winterbottom.

Referee: Giorgio Bernardi (Italy).

Attendance: 92,000.

Scoreline: Lantos 10 minutes, Puskas 17 minutes, Kocsis 19 minutes, Kocsis 57 minutes, Hidegkuti 59 minutes, Toth 63 minutes, Broadis 68 minutes, Puskas 71 minutes.

TEAMS:

England: Gil Merrick, Ron Staniforth, Roger Byrne, Billy Wright (Captain), Syd Owen, Jimmy Dickinson, Peter Harris, Jackie Sewell, Bedford Jezzard, Ivor Broadis, Tom Finney.

Hungary: Gyula Grosics (Captain), Jeno Buzanszky, Mihaly Lantos, Joszef Bozsik, Gyula Lorant, Joszef Zakarias, Jozsef Toth, Sandor Kocsis, Nandor Hidegkuti, Ferenc Puskas, Zoltan Czibor.

It was Bedford Jezzard's England debut.

This was the biggest defeat in England's 90-year football history (and continues to be so to this day). Just four of the England team had survived from the 6–3 slaughter at Wembley in November: Merrick, Wright, Dickinson and Sewell. Fulham centre-forward Bedford Jezzard made a best-forgotten debut, while the unfortunate Peter Harris was winning his second and last cap after a gap of five years. His first cap came in the 2–0 home defeat by the Republic of Ireland in 1949.

Puskas and Kocsis scored two goals each. The Hungarians, leading 3–0 at half-time, were six goals clear and cantering before Ivor Broadis opened the scoring for England. Hungary immediately replied with their seventh goal, scored by Puskas from a pass by Hidegkuti. Hungary's scorers were Puskas (2), Kocsis (2), Lantos, Toth and Hidegkuti. Billy Wright came off with his face as white as his shirt, and looking like a man who had seen a ghost come back to haunt him. As hard as this giant-hearted man tried, he could not get near to suppressing the irrepressible Puskas.

Jack remembers: It was the low point of my football career. I remember going to the 45th Anniversary event with Tom [Finney] and George [Robb] and the disappointment was still there. (Author's Note: Only one other member of the team is still alive today, Gil Merrick – or 'Mister Thirteen', as he became known after the two Hungary games.) **Having said that, I would not have missed the experience for the world because it now means I am part of English international football history, albeit for the wrong reasons. But I was glad to be part of it because none of us had ever witnessed football like it. We knew we had been part of history and we knew we had to change.**

I was the most expensive player in England at the time so God knows what some of the Hungarians would have been worth. To score the

equaliser and briefly give my teammates and the country a glimmer of hope was something else. I remember it as if it was yesterday, I got into some space that had opened up in the box and was able to take Stan's [Mortensen] pass in my stride. But I think we all knew even then that it was meaningless and only temporary parity. You could see in their faces that they didn't mind, they had come to attack and were perfectly confident doing it. They formed little triangles down the field, looked where they were passing and if they couldn't go one way turned and passed in another direction. We had trouble getting the ball. It wasn't a case of underestimating them. We knew they were Olympic champions and unbeaten for nearly 30 games. Walter Winterbottom, our manager, had been to watch them, but nobody could have been prepared for what transpired. I never had to run so much on a football pitch without having the ball. I thought Puskas was an excellent player. I once described him as a 'little pudding with a magic left leg'. Everything worked for him that day and he rightly took his place in history.

Gil Merrick recalls the Wembley match: The game in Budapest was played on an incredibly hot May day, and in those days we knew nothing about nutrition and none of us had taken on enough liquids. Poor old Syd Owen became so dehydrated that he went as rigid as a board and we had to carry him off. A few years ago a TV company were planning a film on Puskas and they wanted to use Wembley as the location. The three remaining members of the England squad, myself, Jackie Sewell and George Robb, were asked to be involved. We agreed but the TV company couldn't raise the funding and the project fell through, which was a shame, I really would have liked to have got involved with that.

During the first half of the match the football played by the Hungarians was a style never seen before; their passing, running and dribbling was amazing and all done at pace with accuracy. At half-time the players had to try and sort it out as the management had little knowledge of tactics! We only lost the second half 1–2, but for the whole game we were under pressure – it was like being at the Alamo. That was the day that the game changed. Hungary had set the standard, even to the extent that they played in a lightweight kit. The nearest I've seen to the way the Hungarians played that day was the Arsenal Premiership winners of 2003–04.

Chapter Nine

FROM HULL CITY
TO NORTHERN
RHODESIA

J**ack recalls:** This was a difficult time for Barbara and I and a vital time
for our son; he had had a critical operation when he was only five
days old and then had an interminable four-month stay in hospital.
He was under constant treatment and care, to get him strong enough to
endure the major surgery he required to give him a normal life.

The end of my time at Aston Villa was the only real low point of my
career. It was obvious that the time had come for me to seriously
consider my career options. My career had in the main always been on
the up, so I felt I still had something to offer a decent side. Let's face it,
by the time I left for Hull City I had a Second Division Championship

medal, a Third Division South Championship medal, an FA Cup-winners' medal, six England caps, five Inter-League medals, two caps for FA Tours of Canada and Australia and had made two FA Cup semi-final appearances in 1954 versus Preston North End and 1958 versus Nottingham Forest, both of whom went on to win the Cup in that year.

Joe Mercer, as the new Aston Villa manager, wanted me to join Doncaster Rovers, where Joe's mate Jackie Bestall was manager. (Author's note: Jackie Bestall managed Doncaster Rovers on four separate occasions: February 1946 to May 1949, April 1959 to August 1960, with Tom Garnett as caretaker manager from February to May 1966, and then once again as caretaker manager in November 1968.)

Joe had already bought Bobby Thomson from Wolverhampton Wanderers for £8,000 to replace me so I had to move on, but I did not fancy Doncaster Rovers or any of the other clubs that had shown interest. Then Bob Brocklebank, the manager of Hull City, came to Birmingham and we had a cup of tea after training. I had not got a clue where Hull was, but I was fed up, mainly due to Paul's medical condition, which meant I was not playing to my maximum, which I was unhappy about, so I decided to get things over and done with quickly. I effectively transferred myself. Knowing that I was not wanted by Joe Mercer, I went into the general office and told them I was leaving to join Hull City. To say they were shocked is an understatement, but my decision suited everyone so it all went off without a hitch.

Paul's surgery was to be carried out in Birmingham. A key factor in Jack joining the Boothferry Park outfit was the fact that Bob Brocklebank agreed that he would be allowed to commute from Birmingham to Hull.

Jack smiles with pride as he remembers that life-giving surgery and an eight-week spell in hospital just before Christmas 1959 finally did the trick, enabling Paul to become a perfectly fit little boy who went on to be a golf professional.

Jack continues: Why would I want to stay at Villa Park? I was only wanted as a stop-gap and that hurt and, in the end, I just had to get away. Who knows, in hindsight perhaps I did make the wrong decision. But, having said that, I have no regrets about the way things worked out in the end.

I joined Hull City in October 1959 at the age of 32, looking forward to a new challenge and a change of luck. It was pleasing for me that I could still command a decent fee: £5,000 was the figure reported in the press and that was a big chunk of the £15,000 the board had given Bob Brocklebank to avoid relegation. The Tigers had gained promotion from Division Three North in 1958–59 and were stranded at the foot of the Second Division.

By Christmas Bob Brocklebank had asked me to take over as skipper, and I was delighted to accept the challenge. I was reported in the press as saying: 'The last four matches the lads have played really well. It's just that nothing has gone our way. The luck has to change some time.' (Author's note: Unfortunately the luck did not change, and after one season in Division Two, Hull City were relegated to the Third Division, winning only five games out of the 20 after Christmas.) Once Paul was fit enough to be discharged from the care of the Birmingham-based consultant I kept my part of the deal with Bob Brocklebank, and in February 1960 I moved into a brand new house near Hull alongside two of my new teammates, Roy Shiner and Ralph Gubbins, who also joined in 1959 from Sheffield

Wednesday and Bolton Wanderers respectively. The three of us became good friends, and funnily enough we all lasted just over a season: I played 44 games and scored eight goals, Roy got eight goals in 22 games before moving to Cheltenham Town, and Ralph scored 10 goals in 45 games before being transferred to Tranmere Rovers. I never really settled and was glad that my stay at Boothferry Park was brief.

Not one of the trio of new forwards enhanced Bob Brocklebank's reputation for 'spotting a good 'un'.

The local press reported: *Tigers manager Bob Brocklebank persuaded 32-year-old Sewell to sign just after 4.00pm for a fee reported to be £5,000.*

No one was more surprised by the move than Villa themselves. Five clubs (of which Doncaster Rovers, Barrow and Workington put in firm offers) were interested in Sewell but he had shown some reluctance to leave Birmingham – about which Villa were by no means unhappy, for Sewell was not on the transfer list, and they will need all their staff in their promotion bid. Chief reason for Sewell's reluctance is that his 18-month-old son has to have an operation, and he does not want to leave Birmingham, where his son's case history is in the hands of a local specialist. To get their man City will permit Sewell to live at Birmingham until the operation has been performed, but then he will move to Hull.

Sewell will partner Bowering on the left wing, with Bill Bradbury switching flanks to resume his old partnership with Doug Clarke. The signing of Jack was in the hope that he could solve Hull's problem, which was best explained by their seven blank score sheets in 11 Second Division games. Despite a tedious train journey, he soon had ready the kind of bright and breezy joke that should give a welcome shot in the arm to dressing-room spirit at Boothferry Park. After being greeted by manager Bob Brocklebank, he became serious – for a few seconds. I asked him how he felt about joining Hull City and the fight that faces him and the rest of the Tigers. 'Well, we're not at the bottom and from what I've seen of Second Division football you have to be pretty bad to get there. Villa are not playing great football but they are at the top. I can tell you this though – I don't like being relegated. Most clubs I have gone to have had a fight on their hands. Everyone knows about the ups and downs of Sheffield Wednesday and last season Villa came down, of course. I want to be playing regularly with a club who are going the other way.'

Although you have to drag it out of him, he knows about clubs going that way too. He sums it all up in five words: I have been very fortunate. He is happy, too, to be back in the game. 'I was getting into a stagnant spell when Mr Brocklebank came along. He offered me the prospect of Second Division football so I took the chance,' he said. One man who is convinced Jackie has done the right thing is his former boss at Villa Park, Eric Houghton: 'You have made a good move,' he said, when Jackie told him he was going to become a Tiger. If his football is stamped with the personality there is in his off-the-field life, it could be that City fans will think the same way.

MEMORABLE GAME

27 DECEMBER 1960
'THIS JACKIE SEWELL IS A REAL JEWEL!'
HULL CITY 3 BRADFORD CITY 0
OFFSIDE DECISIONS, BAD SHOOTING LOSE TIGERS MANY CHANCES

Two goals up after only 10 minutes, Hull City were in command of the game with Bradford City at Boothferry Park from first whistle to last. It was only because their finishing did not match up to the rest of their work and because of a succession of offside decisions, that I will charitably call close affairs, that they did not get an avalanche of goals.

Superbly prompted by Sewell and McMillan, and with Gubbins leading a sparkling attack in fine style, the Tigers poured raid after raid on the Bradford goal. Once more Downie was in good form, however, even though his handling was suspect at times. He certainly saved Bradford on many occasions. Bradford were scarcely in the game and on this form look to have a hard fight ahead of them if they are to escape relegation. Their only answer to City's football this afternoon was a laboured offside trap and some over-robust tackling. Sewell and Price gave the Tigers their quick lead, but there is still a crying need for the Tigers to pep up their finishing. Four minutes from the end Gubbins got a third goal for the Tigers to round off their win.

TEAMS:

Hull City: Fisher, Davidson, Garvey, McMillan, Feasey, Bulless, Clarke, Price, Gubbins, Sewell, King.

Bradford City: Downie, Flockett, Storton, P. Jackson, Currie, Roberts, Duncan, D. Jackson, Layne, Reid, Howard.

Referee: W. Robinson (Darlington).

Scorers: Sewell 5 minutes, Price 10 minutes, Gubbins 86 minutes.

FOR THE RECORD

Hull City were promoted at the end of the 1958–59 season to Division Two having played 46 games, winning 26, losing 11 and drawing nine. In the 1959–60 season they were relegated back to Division Three with a playing record of 42 games, 10 wins, 22 losses and 10 draws. In Jack's final season (1960–61) they won 17, lost 17 and drew 12. Bob Brocklebank resigned in May 1961 to be replaced by Cliff Britton in July.

Although Bob Brocklebank came into Jack's life and career late on, 'the Toff' had a considerable influence on the final stages of what had, up until that time, been one of continual success. Londoner Brocklebank was born in Finchley as one of eight brothers, and he started his football career as an amateur with his hometown team Finchley in the London League. In May 1929 he signed for Aston Villa, but his chances were limited so he signed for Burnley during the 1935–36 season, where he developed into an inside-right, earning the nickname 'the Toff' because of his gentlemanly approach to life and football. Having made 121 appearances for Burnley and scored 33 goals, he moved into management with Chesterfield in September 1945, establishing the club in Division Two before he joining Birmingham City in February 1949. After relegation in 1949–50 to Division Two, Brocklebank began to rebuild the side but resigned in 1954 just six months before they were promoted back to the top flight. He worked as a scout for West Bromwich Albion from October 1954 to March 1955 until he was appointed manager at Hull City. Once more he suffered relegation in his first full season as Hull finished bottom of Division Two in 1955–56. He managed to get the Tigers back up three years later from the newly formed Division Three but they were relegated the following season, which resulted in Brocklebank's resignation in May

1961 because he was frustrated at being unable to guide them straight back up. He had one last fling at management with Bradford City before leaving in October 1964 to retire to Brixham, where he died in September 1981 aged 73.

Jack recalls: I left Hull City on something of a low when I effectively fell out with the Needler brothers, who were on the board. (Author's note: Harold, John and George Henry Needler came from a humble background and through hard work and an element of luck found fortune through their business background, which embraced building, development and construction materials. They became associated with Hull City at the beginning of the 1950s and their influence continued – with Harold's son Christopher prominent – into the 1990s. By the mid-1950s the Needler family had effective control of the club and Harold was installed as chairman of the club.) **Initially I had hoped to go over to Africa for a short-term coaching assignment in the summer of 1960 and then return to England for the new season, which had been approved by the manager, Bob Brocklebank. This idea did not go down well and I was told that if I went then the club would not pay my summer wages. I was not prepared to be 'blackmailed' and said I was going, so they gave me a free transfer. So there I was in Hull and needing to get out to Northern Rhodesia – I sold everything, all my furniture, everything, and travelled down to Nottingham in my maroon Ford Anglia with a grey top. This was a prestige car in the early 1960s, which was reflected in the price I got for it – £900 cash!**

I drew out all my savings from the National Westminster Bank (as it was then), got into a taxi for London, caught the train to the airport and I was away.

Jack left Boothferry Park a very disgruntled man, never dreaming what was in store for him after accepting the offer of a three-month coaching appointment with the City of Lusaka club.

As well as being a player (inside-right, of course), I was also coach, trainer, team selector and father confessor to a newly formed team, which was a mixture of native Africans and Europeans, who included Blackpool's Alan Burrows and Bishop Auckland's George Sharpe. In that first season we finished runners-up in the League and I scored 20 goals in the 16 games.

The three-month trip to Northern Rhodesia looked like a way of filling the empty summer months. After that prospects looked bleak. The likeliest possibility was a hunt for a job and a place as a part-time professional in non-League football. However, things changed for the better, as reported in the local press at the time:

Now, the future for the Sewell family looks as rosy as anything that could be envisaged. The City of Lusaka club cannot wait for Jackie to return to them and he can choose from a number of offers of jobs. Barbara, his wife and their son, Paul, who have been staying in Nottingham while he has been in Lusaka, will join him on this massive adventure. Before them stretches the quick hustle of settling their affairs in England before they return to Rhodesia in September.

Jackie decided to emigrate to Northern Rhodesia in September 1960, moving from the obscurity of life in the Third Division in England to the top of the tree in Rhodesia, where the game was in its infancy but enjoying the kind of boom English football experienced immediately after World War Two.

Jack recalls: It was quite a culture shock for me when I stepped off the plane, a four-prop BOAC Britannia, on the dirt strip that passed for Lusaka International Airport. I had been recruited to help set up and coach football in what was then Northern Rhodesia. I now realise that the sort of reception I received was usually reserved for visiting royalty.

I was soon brought back down to earth from any feelings of majesty when I got down on the job with the players on the pitch. The black players did not have any boots and played in their bare feet. Also they would not tackle the white players. When I asked them why, they said 'No Boss, don't want to hurt the white man.'

At the age of 33 I knew I was entering the end of my so-called illustrious career, and therefore I thought I had seen it all. But Africa was to offer up a whole host of new challenges. First of all I had to get my new players properly shod – and then teach them that black or white they had to tackle the opposition and had to pass the ball to their own teammates instead of kicking it down the field as hard as they could. They had boundless energy and enthusiasm, and beyond that I could see some natural talent. I knew I could work with the Africans and I soon fell in love with their beautiful country. Just a few weeks previously I had been at Hull City and now there I was in Africa, sitting on the verandah in the evening sun, a drink in one hand, looking out over this amazing landscape. It was incredible and so, so different!

Little did I know that this was the beginning of an African adventure that would last well into the 1970s. In 1961 the country was under British colonial rule, but the indigenous population were getting restless, demanding independence and understandably tensions were running high. Sport and football in particular was seen as a way of breeding multi-racial harmony, so my role to pioneer the professional Rhodesia and Nyasaland Football League on behalf of the City of Lusaka Football Club had significant political overtones.

I worked for a while under a cloud of suspicion, with the African Lusaka Football Association seeing me as little more than a propaganda tool for the white-dominated United Freedom Party, but as far as I was concerned I was only there to play football. Within three months as their player-coach the City of Lusaka team claimed victory in the final of the Castle Cup. A year later I returned to settle in the country together with Barbara and Paul to begin a most remarkable period in my life. Once I made the decision to stay I threw myself into the task of rebuilding a multi-racial football team, and even today I can still reel off the almost unpronounceable names of the players who won trophy after trophy: Amos Mushipe, Peter Mulenga, Lucas Bwalaya and thankfully the more easily pronounced Neville Oliver and Tony Petts.

It was with great pride that in 1964 I was chosen to be captain of the Zambia (Northern Rhodesia) national side. Zambia had won its independence and, as part of the celebrations, a national team was picked to play the Ghana All Stars in Lusaka. Unfortunately, one of the consequences of independence was the ousting of expatriates from positions of influence, no matter what sphere of life. Zambian officials took over the club and I was pushed into the background, so I took my talents elsewhere to create similar football structures in Zaire and Zimbabwe.

By the time my African adventure had come to a natural conclusion, I had pioneered football in three African countries, establishing the coaching programmes that have now resulted in virtually every current Premier League side having an African contingent of players within their squads.

Jack's 1957 FA Cup Final shirt.

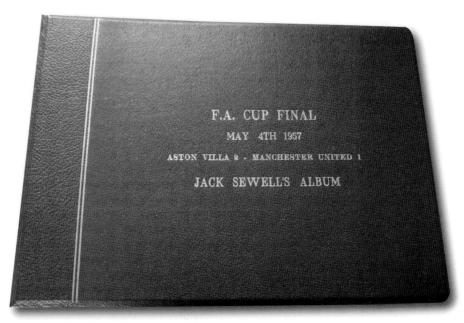

Jack's personalised photograph album.

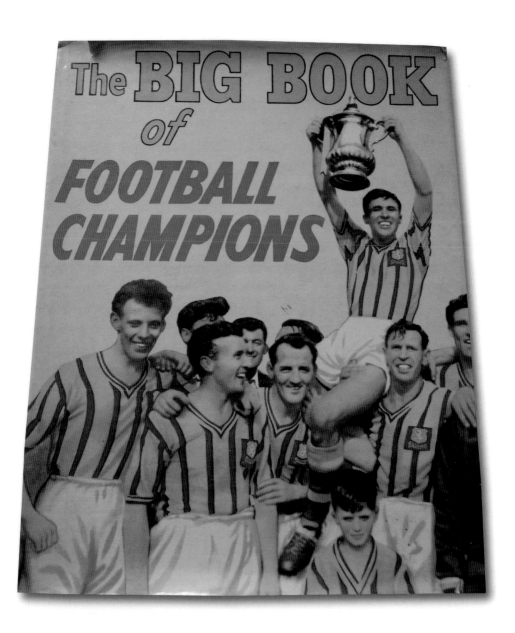

The Aston Villa team on the cover of a popular book.

Jack meets the Queen at Wembley in 1957.

The England party that travelled to Canada in 1950.
Jack is crouching on the far right.

Jack's Football League medals.

The shirt Jack wore playing for the Football League against Eire.

The red England shirt that the players were allowed to keep after a fine performance.

England v Northern Ireland, 14 November 1951. Jack is on the front row, second left.

The England team travelling in Europe, 1952.

Jack with Nat 'the Lion of Vienna' Lofthouse (right).

Jack's England cap from the trip to Austria in 1951–52.

The England team that played Hungary in 1953. Back row, left to right: Alf Ramsey, Billy Wright, Gil Merrick, Harry Johnston, Jimmy Dickinson, Bill Eckersley. Front row, left to right: Stanley Matthews, Ernie Taylor, Stan Mortenson, Jack, George Robb.

Barbara with Paul aged 18 months.

Paul with the Malawi Republic Day Cup, July 1966.

City of Lusaka, 1964.

Receiving the Rothmans Cup from Kenneth Kaunda, 1963.

What a Tiger! Jack in Hull City colours, October 1959.

Jack with the Zambian national team in 1964.

Jack with the Deep River Boys, who were amazed by his small feet.

The *Zambia Daily Mail*, reporting my farewell party in 1974, said: 'As a compassionate person he possessed great qualities for leadership. He was a successful captain and manager for the national team.'

Jack's claim that his legacy in establishing football in Africa is now paying dividends in the Premier League in England is no idle boast. Indeed, his influence has ultimately benefitted teams throughout Europe as well as ensuring that today African national sides can compete on the world football stage. In 1970 FIFA established the African Player of the Year award due to the number of African players who were enjoying careers in the professional game. Modern football has brought African players (some of whom were no more than average in comparison to the local players) and their families new wealth and a very different lifestyle. Nearly every football squad in the major European Leagues – the Premier League (England), La Liga (Spain), Serie A (Italy) and particularly the French Ligue 1 – contains one or more players who originated from Africa.

The first winner of the African Player of the Year award was Salif Keita, who played for St Etienne in France and on the international stage for Mali.

For the next 11 years (1971 to 1982) the award went to players who were playing their football in the emerging African Leagues. As these Leagues became more developed, scouts from the European teams were sent to run the rule over the African League's star players. Many were signed or invited to trials, only to fail because the gap in both the standard of football and lifestyle made it difficult for them. Eventually, the needs of all parties were better understood and we now have a recruitment system which in general benefits the whole of football.

Interestingly, in 2009 Arsenal of the English Premier League has a very sophisticated recruitment, training and development scheme which seems to have its focus on African players. Also in 2009, the wheel has turned full circle with professional coaches from the United Kingdom setting up training camps in Africa, a programme which is being fronted by ex-England international Ian Wright.

Such has been the success of the introduction of African players into the major leagues that the winners of the African Player of the Year award in the last decade have come from the following teams: Arsenal, Parma, Rennes, Liverpool, Real Mallorca, Barcelona, Chelsea and Sevilla, including such Premier League stars as Kanu, Diouf and Drogba, culminating in the 2009 award which went to Emmanuel Adebayor of Manchester City and Togo.

But in the 1960s, in a world which was experiencing changes in every walk of life, an England international footballer's move to Africa was extremely newsworthy, as the *Sports Argus* reported:

SPORTS ARGUS SATURDAY, 10 MARCH 1962
'SOCCER IN THE SUN' BY JACKIE SEWELL

Soccer in Northern Rhodesia may not have the same cash attractions as Italian football, but like my former Aston Villa teammate, Gerry Hitchens, I am enjoying life away from the old country.

There's tremendous scope for the game out here, and I would like to think I have got in on the ground floor. I must confess I was a little doubtful about pulling up my roots when I was first approached by a chap called Donald Lightfoot, who was in charge of Northern Rhodesian Broadcasting. Like myself, Donald originally came from Cumberland, and we had played together in 1945 when I was guesting for Workington. Donald, who helped start semi-professional soccer in Rhodesia, wanted me to act as player-manager for the City of Lusaka team, and after giving it a three-month trial I quickly agreed to make it a permanent job. Let's have a look at life in Northern Rhodesian soccer…

THE JOB

At present I am not a full-timer. I am employed as an insurance representative and my soccer is limited to coaching during the evenings and playing on Sundays. Most of the match arrangements are left to me, and so far as the soccer is concerned I'm in sole charge. If all the managers at home had such an easy life they would be in clover. There's no director trouble out here!

THE PLAYERS

There are several ex-League players floating about. Burrows, who was with Blackpool, was in our team last season, but now he is on the Copperbelt along with Leslie Locke, the ex-Queen's Park Rangers forward. We have six African players in our team. They are polite and are only anxious to learn. They have great potential – all they need is a little coaching.

STANDARD OF PLAY

It's improving all the time. Quite a number of the sides here would give the teams in the lower half of the Third Division a good game. Touring British sides – such as Leicester, Preston, Blackpool and Bolton – have all been given testing games. After all, many of the European players have come from good amateur sides.

THE GROUNDS

Queensmeade, Lusaka's ground, is up to Third Division standard and, in some cases, up to Second Division. Some other grounds are better than Queensmeade and have floodlighting. When Billy Wright was here with Wolves he said that one of the grounds on the Copperbelt was equal to any British standard, and the best in South Africa. After playing on it, I agree.

THE GATES

We were pulling in up to 2,000 towards the end of last season, but the ground is in an unsatisfactory area so far as African support is concerned. They have a long way to travel and there is no public transport. But we are looking for a ground nearer the African area. With the African population topping 70,000, the scope is unlimited. Prices of admission range from 1 shilling to 5 shillings stand seats.

THE LEAGUE SET-UP

Last season there was a Rhodesia and Nyasaland League consisting of five teams – four in the south and only City of Lusaka in the north. This season there is a Southern Rhodesia League and a Northern Rhodesia League. Later on we will play in the National League, with 14 northern clubs competing.

THE PROSPECTS

If there are any young players – or experienced ones – looking for a place, I would try to help them. The one thing I would advise is that they should have a trade, preferably in the building or engineering line. The heat is a problem at first, but you quickly become acclimatised and then it is no trouble.

I find football in the sun is fun.

When I first met Jack at his home to discuss writing this book I was incredibly privileged to see at first hand his incredible collection of personal memorabilia, all of which is carefully stored around his home, either on display or in storage. One of his most prized possessions is a scrapbook; but this no ordinary scrapbook of the type you would buy from a High Street retailer, this one measures about 11in across and 15in in length and is 4in deep. It is has a black hardback cover on which is embossed in gold the legend: JACKIE SEWELL – Notts County – Sheffield Wednesday – Aston Villa – Hull City & England. It is a fantastic testimony to his career in England. It has been meticulously kept to include an array of newspaper cuttings, magazine articles and photographs, all in chronological order.

I reproduce a sample of those scrapbook memories in the form of memorable matches:

MEMORABLE GAME
MALAWI 0 ZAMBIA 6

This match was part of the celebrations for the establishment of the Malawi Republic held at the Central Stadium, Zambia. The president, Dr Kamuza Banda, presented the Republic Trophy to Howard Mwikuta, captain of the winning team, and each player received a Republic Medal, including the losing team members. This victory meant that Zambia had completed the double over Malawi, having won the Independence Cup in 1964.

Levson Lifikilo, a local reporter, remembers: *The opening stages of the game were hectic, with both sides strong and the forwards fast. Although Zambia had more thrust and scoring potential, Malawi's fine performance* had the thousand spectators on tenterhooks until the end. The game was full of good football and had plenty of thrills. By crisp and intelligent combination Malawi gave Zambia a good fight. They kept Zambia under pressure throughout and only clever defending prevented Malawi scoring. But, smooth and fluent in attack and decisive in defence, Zambia proved the better side. They were playing cleverly, closely, and those who appreciate good football had a treat.

Outside-right Mwila put Zambia one up in the ninth minute. His shot went into the net after hitting an upright. Malawi's hero was goalkeeper Kapalamula. His superb saves and anticipation kept the spectators on their toes. Twice he prevented certain goals by diving at full length to stop terrific shots from Mwila. In the 15th minute Mwila scored again to give Zambia a 2–0 lead and increased the lead in the 35th minute. Two minutes later he banged in another goal to give Zambia a 4–0 lead at half-time. The fifth goal came in the 60th minute and this time it was Kalimukwa who scored. Y. Osman broke through for Malawi, but goalkeeper Mwanza brought off a great save. Malawi were now on the attack and tried everything, but the Zambia defence was too good. Both Y. Osman and O. Mkandawire came close but the way to goal was a difficult one. Centre-forward Shawa completed the scoring and Zambia won a thrilling and exciting game 6–0.

MEMORABLE GAME TWO

CITY OF LUSAKA 8 KITWE UNITED 1
'THAT MAN SEWELL!'

Another great display by City of Lusaka skipper Jackie Sewell helped the home team defeat Kitwe United by eight goals to one at Queensmead. Sewell himself scored four of the goals and the whole city team gave one of the best performances of the season in front of a large and enthusiastic crowd.

In the opening minutes of the game the City forwards combined beautifully and launched attack after attack on the Kitwe goal. Playing grand, entertaining football the City forwards clicked well and the ball was swung from one wing to the other. Ngabo had a long run and his flick inside to Sewell saw Ngosa make a fine save. Kitwe took some time to settle down and it was 12 minutes before Williams touched the ball in the City goal. But their period of pressure was soon ended by some astute tackling from Mwelwa and some big clearances. After Felton had slammed high over the bar from 25 yards, City took the lead in the 21st minute. Ngabo took a well-placed corner and Sewell rocketed the ball into the roof of the net.

Within a minute Ngosa saved brilliantly to avert another goal, but City still piled on the pressure and in the 26th minute went further ahead. Again the goal came from a corner and this time Sewell, after seeing Ngosa brilliantly push a tremendous shot round the post, got up to nod the ball well wide of the goalkeeper. Playing attractive soccer, City dominated the play, but Kitwe came back determinedly and Williams was in action against a couple of rasping shots from Tenthzni. One minute from the interval City almost got a third when Felton crashed the ball against the crossbar with Ngosa well beaten. Kitwe set the pattern at the opening of the second half and a good run by Kapembwe ended with his hard, rising shot clipping the edge of the crossbar. But the City defence covered well and with Mwelwa again prominent any likely looking Kitwe attacks were repulsed. In the 56th minute a fine bout of passing between the City forwards brought their third goal. Sewell passed inside to Felton, who put Simukoko away with a perfect pass. Simukoko cut in and shot hard. Caimfutumba, in attempting to clear, deflected the ball past *his own 'keeper. Seconds later Ngosa saved a piledriver from Simukoko, but in the 59th minute Bwalya scored after some neat play by Felton and Ngaba.*

One minute later the Kitwe defence was rocked again. Oliver placed a free kick perfectly for Sewell to nip between the Kitwe full-backs and shoot into the corner of the net. Those three quick goals did not deter the visitors, who in spite of their deficit kept trying to play good football. Kapembwe's persistence was rewarded in the 71st minute when Kitwe were awarded a penalty for a foul by Mwelwa and the winger easily netted. This goal failed to inspire the Kitwe team to greater efforts, however, and it was City who came storming back to score again in the 74th minute. Sewell took a free-kick 40 yards out and placed it perfectly for Bwalya to flick the ball wide of Ngosa. Two minutes later Ngabo got a well-deserved goal. Felton put him away and his superior speed left Mpundu standing. Racing towards goal he was cut off by Nyendwa, but in the ensuing struggle for the ball Ngabo prodded it wide of the full-back and the unfortunate Ngosa. Once again the City scoring came in spells, and in the 78th minute Sewell capped a fine performance with a brilliant goal. He dribbled his way past the Kitwe wing-half before completely deceiving Chimfutumba and then walking the ball into the net past the surprised Ngosa. In this fine game, thoroughly enjoyed by the large crowd, the whole City team played well with schemer Sewell again the brains of a forward line in which Bwalya regained much of his old sparkle. The front line blended well and kept the Kitwe defence on the move with their intelligent play. For the visitors, Ngosa had a fine game in goal with Chimfutumba prominent at centre-half. Best of the forwards were Kapimbwe and Tenthani.

This match report is an excellent example of the football reports which are contained in Jack's scrapbook, and the scoring exploits of Jack and his team are well documented.

From 1961 to 1965 in Northern Rhodesia the prestigious trophy was the Castle Cup. City of Lusaka won the Castle Cup in 1961, its inaugural year, and then again in 1964 when they beat Mufulira Blackpool 2–1:

1964 CITY OF LUSAKA 2–1 MUFULIRA BLACKPOOL
'SEWELL'S CITY SLICKERS CUP WIN OVER BLACKPOOL'

City of Lusaka are Castle Cup winners of 1964. They beat Mufulira Blackpool by two goals to one at Hammarskjoeld Stadium, Ndola, in the Northern Zone Final, and carry the trophy back to the capital in triumph.

And another record was shattered today at this great stadium. An official estimation puts the attendance figure at 8,000 – and what a massive roar issued from thousands of throats and rolled across the turf when City's centre-forward Twetson Magwenzi headed a brilliant winner for the Midlanders from a precision cross from Faya Swana in the 74th minute. A great occasion and a great triumph for skipper Jackie Sewell's side, who add today's victory to their 1961 win in the all-Rhodesia Final against Bulawayo City. But this Final won't go down in Northern Rhodesia's soccer annals as one to be remembered for shining deeds or heroic endeavour.

If anybody made an impression it was 'Big' Juma Chipeta, Lusaka's powerhouse inside-right. With panther-like speed he rampaged through Blackpool's defence, and the opening goal of the match was an unstoppable rising shot from his boot in the 38th minute. No, this was not a game for the connoisseur. It was hard, but devoid of craft or imagination. The ball was in the air too much. The measure of City's superiority was at wing-half, where Edward Zulu and Amos Mushipe ran the show and played with a better understanding than their Blackpool counterparts. The outstanding man on the Mufulira side was centre-half Sebastian Chilekwa, who virtually played Twetson out of the game. Twetson could have probably scored twice in the first half if he hadn't held on to the ball for too long, allowing Chilekwa to rob him. City led 1–0 at the interval through Juma's goal, and continued to have the better of the play. Blackpool's forwards saw very little of the ball, and not once did the halves initiate a move which led to a chance. Their single goal, which levelled the scores in the 63rd minute, was a combination of two inevitable factors: the inevitability that their long up-the-middle ball would pay off at least once, and the inevitability that City's bundle-of-nerves goalkeeper, Bwalya, would make at least one fatal error. Left-half John Chibamba sent a long ball up the middle for centre-forward Dreamwell Chibungo to burst clear of the defence. The little Blackpool man drew Bwalya out of his goal, then calmly flicked the ball over Bwalya's head.

For a few minutes after this Blackpool's spirit flared up. But they never looked like producing another goal, and it was City who kept plugging the ball into the Blackpool penalty area.

In the 74th minute Swana rounded the Mufulira captain and left-back Morgan Siame, and flashed a curling shot into the goalmouth. Mufulira's 'keeper, Sabu, could have cut it out, but a defender was in position to head clear.

Mr Andrew Mutumba, Under Minister for the Western Province, was guest of honour.

City of Lusaka failed to retain the trophy in 1965 when they were runners-up to Mufulira Wanderers, losing 5–2 after extra-time.

Note that winners of this trophy did not always enter the African Cup-Winners' Cup, an entry often reserved for the winners of the Champion of Champions' Cup (usually contested between four clubs).

The Northern Rhodesian Challenge Cup, as it was called before independence, was only competed for by all-white teams and was renamed the BAT Challenge Cup during the period 1962 to 1968. City of Lusaka won the trophy in 1962 and 1963.

MEMORABLE GAME THREE

'NOTHERN RHODESIA CHALLENGE CUP FINAL'

Jackie Sewell and his City of Lusaka teammates treated the season's biggest Queensmead crowd of 2,100 to a sparkling display of football yesterday to romp home in the Northern Rhodesia Challenge Cup Final against Broken Hill Warriors 8–2. After the teams were level at 1–1 at half-time, three quick goals on the resumption turned the game in City's favour. Sewell finished the game with a personal tally of five goals.

In the semi-final match at Queensmead the previous week, City gave a lethargic display and scraped home against Mufulira Wanderers Reserves by the only goal, scored by Sewell.

The Challenge Cup was presented by the Governor, Sir Evelyn Hone.

In 1953, the Federation of Rhodesia and Nyasaland joined Northern and Southern Rhodesia with Nyasaland. This action was undertaken despite opposition from a sizeable minority of Africans, who demonstrated against it in 1960–61. Northern Rhodesia was the centre of much of the turmoil and crisis characterizing the federation in its last years. Initially, Harry Mwaanga Nkumbula's African National Congress (ANC) led the campaign that Kenneth Kaunda's United National Independence Party (UNIP) subsequently took up.

In January 1964, Kenneth Kaunda won the first and only election for Prime Minister of Northern Rhodesia. The Colonial Governor, Sir Evelyn Hone, was very close to Kaunda and urged him to go for the post. Soon afterwards there was an uprising in the north of the country known as the Lumpa Uprising, which was led by Alice Lenshina. She was a self-proclaimed prophetess who claimed that she had had a visitation from an angel telling her to liberate the people. Many followed her and fought the authorities to the death – men, women and children alike. She continued despite pleas from her own brother to give herself up. This was Kenneth Kaunda's first internal conflict as leader of the nation.

A two-stage election held in October and December 1962 resulted in an African majority in the legislative council and an uneasy coalition between the two African nationalist parties. The council passed resolutions calling for Northern Rhodesia's secession from the federation and demanding full internal self-government under a new constitution and a new National Assembly based on a broader, more democratic franchise. The federation was dissolved on 31 December 1963, and Northern Rhodesia became the Republic of Zambia on 24 October 1964, with Kaunda as the first president.

Jackie's contacts meant that on occasions British sides visited Africa, which enabled him to measure his team's progress and give the game much--needed publicity. One such game was when Dundee United visited. The game was played at the Rhokana Stadium in front of 4,000 fans against an Invitation Northern Rhodesian XI, which included Freddie Goodwin of Leeds United and Phil Woosnam from Aston Villa. Dundee won 4–3. The scorers for Dundee were Gillespie (2), Sabu (own-goal) and Irvine, and the scorers for Northern Rhodesia were Sewell (2) and Goodwin.

Jack holds an unusual record for being 'capped' at international level on two continents, as his performances for City of Lusaka soon became acknowledged and he was selected to play for Northern Rhodesia. In his first season as an African international he helped them win the Levy Cup, which was an annual fixture against Southern Rhodesia.

MEMORABLE MATCH FOUR
NORTHERN RHODESIA 4 SOUTHERN RHODESIA 1

This was the second leg, played at the Kafubu Stadium in Luanshya. Northern Rhodesia won the Cup on a 5–2 aggregate score having drawn the previous game 1–1. The first leg was held the day before at Gabbitas Stadium, Nchanga. A crowd of 3,500 saw Laing (2), Pencil and Mizzi score for the North, while Finch replied for the South.

Mr James I. Reid, general manager of Roan Antelope Copper Mine, was guest of honour as the mine was located in Luanshya.

Jack remembers: Even though I was an established international, I still had to go through trials just like the other players. We had a trip to Nyasaland planned together with 10 days concentrated coaching at Mulungushi, for which the players were keen to get selected. The trials were no different to normal soccer trials. The core of the A team were remnants of the previous year's side, and for the record won 2–0, but several changes were made at half-time, with several substitutes brought in and positional switches introduced.

In the days after the trial game, the national selectors chose the following Northern Rhodesia side:

Number	Name	Club
1	Amato	Ndola United
2	Banda	Rhokana United
3	Bent	Broken Hill Warriors
4	Chimbala	Broken Hill Warriors
5	Chifutu	Rhokana United
6	Emment	Kitwe United
7	Howard	Bancroft Blades
8	Juma	City of Lusaka
9	Kunda	Mufulira Wanderers
10	Musonda	Mufulira Wanderers
11	Mwanza	Mufulira Wanderers
12	Mizzi	Broken Hill Warriors
13	Pencil	Rhokana United
14	Sewell (Captain)	City of Lusaka
15	Sikazwe	Mufulira Wanderers

All the triallists, plus Charma and Chime of Rhikana United and Kabasa and Chirwa of Mufulira Blackpool, were invited to attend the Mulungushi training course from June 1–12.

The local press reported: *Without a doubt Northern Rhodesia has the talent to produce one of the strongest football sides in Africa for, despite the expected displays of individuality, the basic skills were there, needing only to be fitted together. Notable absentees through injuries were Williams and Juma from City of Lusaka and Kenny Banda of Roan, who were nevertheless considered for the national side.*

The match itself took a quarter of an hour to settle down, with Sewell seeing his neat cross from the right wing headed down by Kunda but well saved by Mwanza. Mizzi looked dangerous on the left wing but was well contained by Bent, playing in an unusual right-back position.

The A team controlled midfield play in the first half, with Amato particularly strong. Sewell played his best game of the season and Emment was steady on the right wing.

For the B team, Haylen and Pencil showed up well in the first half, but Stephen had little opportunity to move. A pass through the middle by Sewell saw Mizzi with a chance but Mwanza again saved well. There were no goals by half-time.

Chimbala was changed to the B team and Stephen to the A team to give both of them an opportunity to see more of the ball. This worked well for Chimbala was kept busy and Stephen was unlucky on several occasions to see his shots go wide or be blocked.

The best move of the match saw Sewell beat three men before crossing to Mizzi, whose shot hit the post but rebounded into the net off Chimbala.

FOR THE RECORD

NORTHERN RHODESIA 5 NYASALAND 1
OCTOBER 1963
HAMMARKSKJOELD STADIUM, NDOLA

Scorers: Northern Rhodesia: Sewell (3) Albert Heylen (2).
Nyasaland: Bweya.

In 1964 the local newspaper *The Star* selected its All-Star team:

Goalkeeper: *Tolomeo MWANZA (Mufulira Wanderers), the best of the showboat goalies in the NFL. Coming up fast on the outside is Happy Malama of the Roan Antelopes. Mwanza, known as 'Juva', is 23. He is 5ft 6ins and 159lbs.*

Right-back: *Howard MWIKUTA (Bancroft Blades) is one of the strong, tough men of any Zambia team. At 23 he looks forward to a long and illustrious future with the Zambia XI.*

Left-back: *Fred BENT (Broken Hill Warriors) is a keen young player who helped Northern Rhodesia win the Ufulu Cup in Malawi in July. Although he has been ill suddenly on several occasions, the 24-year-old railroader is one of Zambia's most dependable backs.*

Right-half: *Juma CHIPETA (City of Lusaka) is Lusaka's most crowd-pleasing player. Although switched to inside-right for a period, his position is at wing-half. He played for Northern Rhodesia in Malawi.*

Centre-half: *Kenny BANDA (Roan Antelopes) is a key man in the Roan defence, and although injured at the tail-end of the season he remains number one in the middle position.*

Left-half: *George SIKAZWE (Mufulira Wanderers) ace wing-half of the All-Star Wanderers who won both the Challenge and Heinrich Cups this year. Although getting along in years, he is still a force to be reckoned with in NFL football.*

Outside-right: *Emment KAPENGWE (Kitwe United) is first choice at this position, although many fans would swear by Kenneth Simwanza. But* *playing for the lowly Kitwe he has had to carry the load by himself. One of the few bright lights in the Independence Kwacha Cup matches.*

Inside-right: *Samuel NDHLOVU (Mufulira Wanderers) is better known as 'Zoom'. The quick-thinking captain of the Wanderers is playing at his best this year and neatly balances the forward line. He has been playing top-flight football for almost 10 years.*

(Author's note: Ndhlovu was born in Mufulira in 1937 and played his club football solely for his local team. He was unfortunate enough to experience segregation in colonial Northern Rhodesia where two Leagues ran side by side – one for whites and the other for Africans – making many appearances for the national team and also featuring for the mixed team after Northern Rhodesia got its independence and became Zambia in October 1964.

His skill on the ball, close control and deadly shooting were a marvel to witness and he earned himself the nickname 'Zoom' because of the way he would meander past defenders.)

Centre-forward: *Willie KUNDA (Mufulira Wanderers) is a teenage wonder and anywhere near the goal is a terrible threat. Despite the attention given to him by hard-hitting and rough defencemen he hangs in there and is a constant danger.*

Inside-left: *Jackie SEWELL (City of Lusaka) the former English international is the only European on the All-Star team. At 37 he is near the end of the trail, but 'the Schemer' remains a constant threat.*

Outside-left: *Mizzi NKANDAWIRE (Broken Hill Warriors) is not what he once was and many might fault this selection, but he is still one of the most dangerous men in the NFL. The impossible shot he made in Luanshya against Roan will be a reminder that when he wants to be can be the best.*

Managers of the Year: Dougie Sammons of the Mufulira Wanderers and Jackie Sewell share managing honours this year in Zambia. Jackie Sewell because City of Lusaka had so much to overcome in winning the Castle Cup and the Rothman Trophy. Despite the loss of players, both through injury and through quitting, despite having to shuffle the line up constantly, City of Lusaka came through to win the NFL. Dougie Sammons, because he has coached the superb men of Mufulira to two Championships, the Heinrich and the Challenge Cups. He managed the Rhodesian side in winning the Ufulu Cup in Malawi in July and the Zambia side in defeat in Kwacha Cup matches in October.

Jackie recalls the Kwacha Cup in October 1964: Overconfidence and lack of teamwork led to the disaster at the Kwacha Cup matches. Our players were unimpressed with Kenya and Uganda and only woke up after two defeats during the final game when we almost beat the Ghana XI. We were not aggressive enough. We were sitting back and waiting for the ball while the other teams went after the ball. It was frustrating because in the last match we came alive. People accused the team of being out of condition and tired, but you show me any side that goes full tilt for 90 minutes. What we lacked was not playing together often enough so that we could cover each other all the time. The way for Zambia to have a world-class team is to take a group of players and train them constantly, with plenty of schooling in the fundamentals of football for several years, just like Ghana.

The tournament was reported as follows: *Zambia's football heroes' faces were the colour of their new football jerseys – green – after last week's debacle. After walking away with the Ufulu Cup in Malawi in July, without allowing a score, Zambia's mighty men decided that the second-rate teams that came to play in Zambia's own Kwacha Cup competition could be beaten without a struggle.*

UFULU CUP MATCHES

Northern Rhodesia 5 Malawi 0 (Sewell (3) Kunda(2))
Northern Rhodesia 3 Tanganyika 0 (Sewell, Pencil, Mizzi)

Northern Rhodesia: Mwanza (Goalkeeper) Howard (Right full-back) Bent (Left full-back) Sikazwe (Right half-back) Banda (Centre half-back) Juma (Left half-back) Chifita (Outside-right) Pencil (Inside-right) Kunda (Centre-forward) Sewell (Inside-left) Mizzi (Outside-left).

But football games are won on the field of play, and Zambia's footballers left their skills somewhere along the way.

After two defeats against Kenya and Uganda, the Lusaka fans finally saw their national team at its best against the 'show boys' from Ghana.

Ghana's second team, who changed jerseys at half-time, from baby blue to white, played a 'rock 'em, sock 'em game'. It was their finishing power more than their all-round performance that brought them victory.

Jackie Sewell played one of his most brilliant games. During the previous games the ageing football warrior had shown little and it was thought that he would not be chosen for the final game. But, for once, the coaches were right and at centre-forward he was the artful schemer of old. Needle-sharp passes and hustle made him an always dangerous demon.

Zambia's first goal came from a beautiful header by Sewell with the game only minutes old. The only other European on the national team, Robertson of Broken Hill, was no asset to Zambia. Although he tried hard at inside-right, there was little doubt that Ginger Pencil of Roan would have been a better choice. He would not have been so readily rough-housed by the Ghana team.

Robertson was injured in the final minutes of play and never returned to action. Except for the glaring weakness in the goal where Sabu replaced Chimbala, Zambia's defence was sterling. But Sabu was enough to ruin the efforts of the team as he misjudged four goals which could have been caught.

Standings

	P	W	L	D	F	A	Pts
GHANA	3	3	0	0	13	4	6
UGANDA	3	2	1	0	5	4	4
KENYA	3	1	2	0	6	12	2
ZAMBIA	3	0	3	0	5	9	0

In the mid-1960s African football had a long way to go and Jackie said as much; there was plenty of potential and basically most of the locals were natural soccer players, but in those days professional football was a long way off.

No one can calculate the impact Jackie had on establishing soccer in Africa, but clearly, along with other Europeans, at the time he was a major influence in creating awareness of the game and how to play it in the right manner. Certainly within the African countries at the time his ability and influence was in demand, for in October 1965 he was appointed trainer/coach for the Zambian soccer XI for its tour of Uganda.

I remember there was a reception given by our sponsors BAT (British American Tobacco) at the Savoy Hotel in Ndola, and at a press conference I pronounced: 'It is unfortunate that the side could not have had more practice together before the trip. The only time they have met since the match against Kenya two weeks ago was this afternoon (12 October), when a short training session was held.'

The issue of getting players together for international matches was as valid in 1965 as it is today, and of course there are always two sides to the argument: the football side and the administrative view. At that press conference John Kelly, president of the Zambia Football Association, said that the side had played as a team on numerous occasions and he was optimistic about Zambia's chances.

I remember it was a punishing schedule. We left on a chartered flight at 7.20am on Wednesday 13 October and we arrived at Entebbe later in the afternoon. Our first match was at Kampala on the Saturday against Uganda. After a day's rest we played them, again in Kampala, and we got back to Zambia on the Wednesday at 4pm.

Football in Africa at that time was seen as being very powerful from a political point of view, and we were sent off with a message from President Kaunda ringing in our ears: 'Be a credit to your country and show what true sportsmanship means'. Kaunda had also sent a telegram to the president of Uganda, stating 'I commend the team to Uganda. Their visit will serve to strengthen the brotherly ties between our countries.'

10

Chapter Ten

REFLECTIONS

NO PLACE FOR STAN MATTHEWS

I played in six full internationals for England alongside some of the legends of English football, but who was the best in each position? Well, it is a difficult decision but for me this would be my side, which with all modesty includes myself:

Goalkeeper:	Gil Merrick	Birmingham City
Right-back:	Alf Ramsey	Tottenham Hotspur
Left-back:	Bill Eckersley	Blackburn Rovers
Right-half:	Billy Wright	Wolverhampton Wanderers
Centre-half:	Jack Froggatt	Portsmouth
Left-half:	Jimmy Dickinson	Portsmouth
Outside-right:	Tom Finney	Preston North End

Inside-right:	Jackie Sewell	
Centre-forward:	Nat Lofthouse	Bolton Wanderers
Inside-left:	Eddie Baily	Tottenham Hotspur
Outside-left:	Billy Elliott	Sunderland

WHO WAS LEON LEUTY?

As a footballer I plied my trade with some great clubs and was incredibly fortunate to experience first-hand the talents of some great players, not all of whom became household names. My all-stars XI from the clubs I played for, excluding myself on this occasion, would be:

Goalkeeper:	Gordon Bradley	Notts County
Right-back:	Stan Lynn	Aston Villa
Left-back:	Peter Aldis	Aston Villa
Right-half:	Eddie Gannon	Notts County
Centre-half:	Leon Leuty	Notts County
Left-half:	Harry Adamson	Notts County
Outside-right:	Alan Finney	Sheffield Wednesday
Inside-right:	Albert Quixall	Sheffield Wednesday
Centre-forward:	Tommy Lawton	Notts County
Inside-left:	Redfern Froggatt	Sheffield Wednesday
Outside-left:	Peter McParland	Aston Villa

Although not a household name, Leon Leuty was quite a star of his day. He joined Notts County from Bradford City for £25,000. Previously he had played for Derby County, with whom he had won an FA Cup-winners' medal in 1946. Leon died tragically in 1955 of leukaemia. He was a great centre-half against whom no centre-forward enjoyed playing.

MODERN-DAY HEROES

These days I watch most of my football on the television and I enjoy the modern game. A lot of people ask me to compare the current games against what it was like in my day – well, it is impossible to compare because everything is different: the ball, boots, kit, tactics, fitness and so on. However, the player who always reminds me of myself on the pitch from the Premier League is Wayne Rooney because of his energy and eye for goal. In the recent past it was Jimmy Greaves – his movement around the penalty area and his ratio of goals scored from within the goal area was just like me!

BIG TRANSFER HOODOO

When I made the record transfer move to Sheffield Wednesday the amount of press coverage was exceptional – nothing compared to what goes on these days with the tabloids, but nevertheless in those days it was big news and the newspapers would not let it go. It ran for weeks as the journalists looked at the implications of the fee size from every conceivable angle. I was supposed to be a player with a difference, a 'Soccer Cinderella' (which one hack called me, presumably because the whole situation had been played out as a pantomime) with a golden chip on my shoulder. There was no chip on my shoulder and I certainly didn't live in any other world than the one that was placed before me. The fans had preconceived ideas about me, fuelled by the press, which suited their partisan views when I made a bad pass or did something wrong. I would hear their shouts of 'Big Head' particularly, but I got called a few other choice things too. I hate to think what they shout at today's big-money transfer stars!

My attitude was to simply take whatever was given because whatever I did or said would not change things. I had to be true to myself and do my very best on the field as a footballer. Naturally I was a marked man, a player who was supposed never to make a mistake. For the money the club had paid for me, as far as the home fans were concerned, I was expected to perform miracles every time I got the ball. It got really tedious. My job was to play football and I can safely say without fear of contradiction that in virtually every game I played in I tried to perform to the best of my ability.

My principles were driven into me from a very early age in a number of ways. A small mining village upbringing soon gives you the judgement to know what is really important in life. Being surrounded by miners ensured you had what they call today 'a work ethic'. When I was a lad I did not support a particular team, but I remember when I sat with my Dad filling in the weekly football pools coupon on a Thursday night, I thought that one day I would like to play for one of the teams listed.

In those days there was a saying that the best players came from mining villages because young men would much rather earn their living at football than follow their fathers down the pits. Funnily enough, saying that reminds me that in my case I had to work in the mine so that I could play football – my job as a milk boy didn't give me any free time on a Saturday, but once I had moved to working in the local pit I got weekends off, which meant I could play football. My commitment to being a footballer was total, which made the suggestions that I was a 'glamour boy' or a 'magician' that could produce goals out of the blue like a conjuror pulling rabbits from out of a hat hard to take. I had never dreamed of being transferred for large sums of money, the transfer market was wholly responsible for that issue. I never asked for a transfer in my life, even when I left Villa for Hull!

Some players used transfers in my day to get a nice 'cut on the side', which was happening on a frequent basis when football clubs were prepared to break the rules of the Football Association regarding transfers of players from one club to another. None of the clubs who signed me turned a blind eye to these rules, so I made no financial gain from my moves other than those that were allowed under the rules.

When I was transferred to Sheffield Wednesday I was told that County needed the money and I would be doing the club a favour if I agreed to leave, so I did what was asked of me. That was how things were in those days, we respected authority and never thought to question a decision to enhance our own circumstances. Footballers in the 1950s were the property of the club and you were expected to 'toe the line' and do exactly what the club wanted you to do. I was no different. I was told they wanted me to go so I went, and it wasn't until sometime after that I found out the decision divided the board of directors and resulted in one or two resignations.

Footballers then, and I guess it is still true today, were never given the credence to have emotions about the changes imposed on their professional careers. I felt that the cares of the world had been placed on my shoulders – the future of the oldest football club in England rested on my decision. My family were as upset as I was. When my mother heard the news she burst into tears. Dad couldn't eat for days as they realised that I was being put on the spot. I felt like a pawn in a game of chess, knowing I was in the game but with very little influence on the outcome of it.

My colleague and best friend, Tommy Lawton, straightened me out. He had already experienced what I was going through and simply told me that if Sheffield Wednesday wanted to spend that kind of money on me then that was their worry and not mine. With that he took me home, opened a bottle of champagne to celebrate and funnily enough I felt a lot better after that evening!

Tommy was a very straightforward man and knew that in my mind I was worried about the supposed 'hoodoo' which surrounded players who seem to fail for their new clubs after big-money moves. Strangely enough, there were a number of hoodoos around in football in the 1950s, the biggest one being the so-called 'Wembley Hoodoo'. I think it started with Walley Barnes (Arsenal) in 1952 and then there was Jimmy Meadows (Manchester City, 1955), Bert Trautmann (Manchester City, 1956) and Ray Wood (Manchester United, 1957). I am never likely to forget that one as it was sickening but a total accident. It was the way the game was played in those days. Anyway, it carried on with Roy Dwight (Nottingham Forest, 1959) and Dave Whelan (Blackburn Rovers, 1960), and I am sure there were others.

But the hoodoo that was waiting for me was the 'big transfer hoodoo'. Trevor Ford had moved to Cardiff City for £30,000 from

Sunderland after a previous move for the same money from Aston Villa, and, according to the press, Trevor did not 'look a happy man since the move'. Tommy's take was that Ford was a pretty miserable character anyway and tended to play his football in a similar way. So no problem there then!

The other subject of the 'big transfer hoodoo' was Bryn Jones, who never looked the same player after his transfer from Wolverhampton Wanderers, but according to Tommy that was more to do with the move to London for a Welshman and also that he had been bought to fill the boots of the legendary Alex James, rather than anything related to the size of the transfer fee.

(Author's note: Bryn Jones was with Wolverhampton Wanderers from 1933 to 1938 and in that time scored 52 goals in 163 games. He joined Arsenal at the beginning of the 1938–39 season for the then world record fee of £14,000 and got off to a great start, scoring on his debut against Portsmouth. However, his goalscoring soon dried up and he finished the season with only four goals.)

I can remember a lesser-known victim of the 'big transfer hoodoo' and that was Bill Paterson. Bill was considered to be a great prospect and spent five years with Doncaster Rovers. In 1955 Newcastle United bought him in the hope that he would answer their centre-half problem. Unfortunately for Bill, things did not work out and in three seasons he only made 22 appearances for the Tyneside outfit.

MY BEST MAN

Les Smith began his playing career with Wolves in 1945 and played in Wolves' legendary 3–2 victory over the Hungarian team Honved in December 1954.

While at Wolves he was very often the understudy to Wolves legends Jimmy Mullen and Johnny Hancocks, although he never complained and always gave 100 per cent whenever selected. He never asked for a transfer even though he knew he could command a first-team place in virtually any other team in the First Division. So when Villa showed the Molineux club a cheque for £25,000 Les came to Villa Park in 1956 and made the right-wing slot his own.

He was a great success on the right wing, scoring 25 goals in 130 appearances. Les remained a friend well after his playing days were over. They had ended prematurely in 1960 when he was forced to retire due to an Achilles tendon injury. Les married Mavis and they had a son, Nigel, who was 45, and had made Les a grandfather twice over before he died aged 80, when the throat and bowel cancer he had fought off some years earlier returned.

RUB STUDS

'Rub studs' was a dice game by Abbey Corinthian made in conjunction with 'Rubstuds' in the 1950s. The game consisted of two dice with various football terms on them, and they came with instructions which had a score card on the back. It was a promotional item for the football studs company and was endorsed by many leading players, such as Sam Bartram, Tommy Lawton, Billy Steel and Jackie.

There was a time when footballers up and down the country used to throw away their boots when the studs wore out on the moulded soles. That was until Rubstuds – from the Fussells Rubber Company – came along. The advert below appeared in the second edition of *World Soccer* and reads:

Billy Wright recommends Rubstuds. The best football stud is the famous Rubstud. But it must a genuine rubstud – don't be taken in by imitations. Look for the name…Rubstud. If it doesn't say Rubstud, don't buy it. Obtainable from sports shops wearing the Rubstud logo in the window. When the studs on your boots wear down, use Rubstuds. Rubstuds, another great product from Fussells.

TOP GOALSCORERS

I was notified by a friend in January 2006 that I featured in the top 100 goalscorers in the Football League, ranked at 65th equal with Francis Lee, David Herd and Pat Terry with 228 goals.

It does not worry me but if you look at their average season strikes it makes interesting reading, as obviously the more games you play, the greater the opportunity to score goals.

Player	Goals	Seasons	Season Average
Sewell	228	14	16.2
Lee	228	15	15.2
Terry	228	15	15.2
Herd	228	19	12

The top five goalscorers in the analysis referred to were:

Pos	Player	Goals	Seasons	Season Average	Revised Ranking
1	Arthur Rowley	433	18	24.05	Fourth
2	Dixie Dean	379	15	25.26	Second
3	Jimmy Greaves	357	13	27.46	First
4	Steve Bloomer	352	21	16.76	Fifth
5	George Camsell	345	14	24.64	Third

The debate about who was the greatest goalscorer will rage on throughout the decades, and rightly so as there are so many factors to take into account: the division played in, the time in which one played, the quality of the goalkeepers one faced, whether the striker was part of a goalscoring double act. All these factors count but can never be taken into account in a truly objective way. Just imagine what Premier League sides would give for a striker who could guarantee them double figures every season!

My old strike partners, by the way, had an average season strike rate of: Nat Lofthouse – 18.2 and Tommy Lawton – 11.55.

FAMOUS JACKS

I was intrigued to know that I featured on an internet site which listed 100 famous football Jacks. Number one was Jack Charlton of Leeds and England, while I came in at number 75 – and they had the nerve to list me as 'Jackie' not Jack!

Jack's extended playing career ended in 1973, at the age of 46. He returned to the United Kingdom with his family and became a car salesman with

Bristol Street Motors in Nottingham. Nottingham became Jack's adopted home on his return from Africa, and he still lives in a quiet suburb of Nottingham in the neat bungalow he has shared with his wife Barbara, whom he married in December 1957, since 1974. Their marriage was blessed with one child, a son, Paul John, who is a member of the Nottinghamshire Professional Golfers' Association and has recorded victories in the Nottinghamshire Assistants Stroke Play Championship in both 1980 and 1981.

Jack was also a good golfer, getting down to a handicap of four before he was forced to stop playing in 2001 when Barbara became dependent on Jack for her care. In 1992 Barbara developed the first symptoms of Parkinson's disease, and the same year she underwent a mastectomy. Her bad luck continued with two falls, the first of which came at Turkey Airport when she broke a hip and the second at home, which resulted in a broken leg. From 1995 she was confined to a wheelchair. Jack's loyalty to her was incredible and touching as he made normal conversation with the love of his life, even though she did not recognise him from the stranger in the corner writing her husband's biography. Sadly, Barbara passed away in the summer of 2009.